An Idle Tale Becomes Good News

Messages On Lent
And Easter Themes

Herchel H. Sheets

CSS Publishing Company, Inc., Lima, Ohio

Copyright © 2002 by
CSS Publishing Company, Inc.
Lima, Ohio

Scripture quotations are from the *New Revised Standard Version of the Bible*, copyright 1989 by the Division of Christian Education of the National Council of the Churches of Christ in the USA. Used by permission.

Scripture quotations marked (RSV) are from the *Revised Standard Version of the Bible*, copyrighted 1946, 1952 ©, 1971, 1973, by the Division of Christian Education of the National Council of the Churches of Christ in the USA. Used by permission.

Scripture quotations marked (NKJV) are from *The New King James Version*. Copyright © 1979, 1980, 1982, Thomas Nelson Inc., Publishers.

Library of Congress Cataloging-in-Publication Data

Sheets, Herchel H.
  An idle tale becomes good news : messages on Lent and Easter themes / Herchel H. Sheets.
    p. cm.
Includes bibliographical references.
  ISBN 0-7880-1933-3 (pbk. : alk. paper)
  1. Lenten sermons. 2. Easter—Sermons. 3. Sermons, American. I. Title.
  BV4277 .S427 2003
  252'.62—dc21

                        2002015018

For more information about CSS Publishing Company resources, visit our website at www.csspub.com or e-mail us at custserv@csspub.com or call (800) 241-4056.

ISBN 0-7880-1933-3   PRINTED IN U.S.A.

To
Gladys
Randy and Rodney
Melanie and Marsha

Table Of Contents

Foreword

Dr. Herchel Sheets has been a mainstay of Methodism in the North Georgia Conference for over fifty years. His gifts as a pastor, teacher, and administrator are well known among laity and clergy.

In this book of sermons, he shares his preaching skills as we are led on a journey through the sermons of Lent and Easter. Dr. Sheets captures in each message a phrase or object that becomes a platform for us as we examine the richness of the biblical narrative. In doing so we are able to experience the wholeness of the Christian life understood in light of the cross and the open tomb.

Just as early Christians were encouraged by the sustained promise of the resurrection, we too relive these spiritual events each spring and profess anew that God's Kingdom, faith, love, and hope are eternal and imperishable. The Christian life rests on no "idle tale," but on the transforming power of the gospel.

Dr. Sheets writes and preaches out of a deep love for God, an uncompromising devotion to Christ, and a sincere affection for the Church. His sermons can equip us for sharing the ultimate Good News of God's self-giving and saving love.

Bishop G. Lindsey Davis
North Georgia Annual Conference

Preface

When Ralph Waldo Emerson was licensed to preach in the Unitarian community in 1826, he was following in the footsteps of ancestors all the way back to Puritan days. But he served as a pastor (Second Church, Boston) for only three years, from 1829 to 1832. He thereafter attended church services, at least occasionally, and sometimes made notations in his Journal about the services. For instance, on December 10, 1837, he made this comment in his Journal:

> *I cannot hear a sermon without being struck by the fact that amid drowsy series of sentences what a sensation a historical fact, a biographical name, a sharply objective illustration makes! Why will not the preacher heed the admonition of the momentary silence of his congregation (and often what is shown him) that this particular sentence is all they carry away?*[1]

I have thought about that comment as I have explored these Lenten and Easter themes. In each of the following chapters, I have pinpointed something specific related to Jesus' ministry in his final days or in his resurrection appearances. In several instances, the focus is not on something concrete. That is, it is not on something that could be seen or touched. But yet it is something that is definite and precise: Jesus' unspoken prayer for his disciples, the "cup" he did not want to drink, Pilate's wife's dream, the astounding news of Jesus' resurrection that seemed like "an idle tale," Thomas' doubt, and Jesus' word of commission and promise.

Other chapters deal with objects that could have been seen and touched: a jar of ointment, a table, ropes, water, tears, a drug,

9

a curtain, spices, a road, scars. In every instance, something significant was happening. What I have tried to do is to explore those happenings to see the light that is thrown on life and on the Christian message for us today.

When we are dealing with the Cross and the Resurrection, we are at the very heart of the Christian gospel, with so much that deserves our study and thought. The themes dealt with here have developed in my mind across many years of study, preaching, and teaching. I am grateful for the congregations and classes or groups with whom I have had the privilege of sharing these developing thoughts, in various situations and forms. Since my retirement after fifty years of active ministry, I have returned to these themes, explored them anew, and worked at putting them into fresh form to share with others.

I am aware that there is so much more to be said, even about the things I have chosen to discuss. But I pray that the Spirit will use these thoughts to stir the hearts and minds of at least a few people, to bring them closer to God's own heart, and to move them to finer service in the name of Christ.

---

1. Bliss Perry, editor, *The Heart of Emerson's Journal* (New York: Dover Publications, Inc., 1958, 1995), p. 106.

1.

The Set Face

Luke 9:51-56

"He set his face to go to Jerusalem." — Luke 9:51

"He set his face to go to Jerusalem." Looked at in one sense, that is a simple statement about physical movement and direction. But looked at in another sense, it says something also about the intention of his heart, the bent of his soul, the determination of his will.

Persons set their faces toward a great variety of things: a child toward possession of a toy, a youth toward pursuit of an education, an athlete toward excellence in a sport. Faces may be set toward the accumulation of money, the development of a skill, the acquisition of knowledge, the reaching of a position or office, or any number of other ideals or goals.

A Picture Of Purpose

A set face is a picture of purpose. It certifies that one is not a drifter but is moving by virtue of decision and intention.

Leo Tolstoy, in *War and Peace*, tells of a countess coming to the point where she no longer lives but merely eats, drinks, sleeps, or stays awake. In rapid succession, she loses both her husband and her son in death. The shock is so great that she feels herself accidentally forgotten in this world and left without aim or object for her existence. Tolstoy writes, "Life gave her no new impressions ... Her life had no external aims — only a need to exercise her various functions and inclinations was apparent."[1]

11

That is life void of purpose and therefore without direction. Not to be intent on anything, to be committed to nothing, is to leave one's life without management, with everything left to chance and circumstance.

Theologian Paul Tillich was traveling in Europe in 1936, and he wrote in his diary about a dinner conversation with a certain person in which they discussed psychoanalysis and religion. They talked especially about whether the power to fulfill one's own meaning is inherent in a person. His host, Tillich wrote, held that every human being brings "a program" into the world and that the fulfillment of that program is, at the same time, the fulfillment of the meaning of his or her life.[2]

Tillich's host may have been right, but it is not too hard to find persons who seem not to have brought "a program" into the world with them, for they are living without purpose. No dream has ever possessed them; no great ideal has ever mastered them.

But that was not true of the Christ with the set face. Turning toward Jerusalem was not a chance act; it was a deliberate decision. He did it because he had made up his mind about some things. He did not drift or just casually move toward Jerusalem. He moved in that direction with conscious intent. He was not a victim of circumstances, but was acting in freedom and independence.

A set face means a set heart, and such is essential to significant achievement. Drifters never put the human race in their debt. It is only those who have set faces who do that.

A Window On Wisdom

It must be recognized, however, that a set face can bring about undesirable consequences. It does not necessarily herald good things, but may forecast evil and harm. All depends upon the direction in which the face is set.

An extreme and tragic illustration of this is the face that is set on self-destruction. Purpose is present, but the purpose is not commendable. A face may be set in the direction of acquisition, with others figuring in one's purpose only as they contribute to what one wants. That is a set face, but can we really call it good?

A set face may indicate simply that a person is stubborn. A determination has been made to go in a certain direction and one is going to do it regardless. Or the set face may be a vindictive face; it is motivated by the desire to "get even" with or to harm another in some way. Jealousy may be a motivating factor, as may prejudice or ambition or greed or lust. Even the desire for a good time can cause one to have a set face. Intent on enjoying oneself, one sets one's face in the direction of what one believes constitutes thrill, excitement, adventure, enjoyment.

A set face then is not to be considered an end in itself. It is important, but it reflects wisdom only if it is set in the right direction. There were many directions in which Jesus could have set his face, and at other times he had set his face in some of those directions. But always he had been motivated by concern for obedience to the will of God and for the best welfare of his fellow human beings.

At this point in his life, that concern pointed him toward Jerusalem. That was why "he set his face to go to Jerusalem." He was not going in the interest of self-promotion of any kind, nor because of resentment or hatred or lust or the desire for a good time. He was going because he believed God wanted him to go.

That means that his set face is for us a window on wisdom, for the will of God never brings one to moral ruin nor to spiritual decay. It always brings one toward personal wholeness and fulfillment, as well as toward the finest contribution it is possible for one to make to others.

A Call To Courage

We should not be under the illusion, though, that the will of God is always something easy, comfortable, peaceful, or enjoyable. It may be and often is like that, but not always nor inevitably. Jesus could have testified to that. It required courage, as well as commitment to the purposes of God, for him to decide to go to Jerusalem at that particular time. He had already read the sign on the road to Jerusalem and knew that it said, "Proceed at your own risk," yet he was determined to proceed. He was not traveling the road of expediency but of conviction and purpose. He knew there was a cross at the end of that road, but he traveled on anyway.

Britisher John Rogers was the first of a "noble army of martyrs" who suffered under Queen Mary in the sixteenth century. His offense was preaching Protestant doctrines. After more than a year of trials and imprisonments, he was finally burned at the stake in February of 1555. His wife and children spoke to him as he passed on the way to the place of execution, encouraging him to steadfastness. A French ambassador who witnessed the scene wrote that Rogers "went to his death as though it had been his wedding."[3]

The same courage possessed Jesus as he traveled to Jerusalem. Even his disciples were amazed at his courage. The Gospel of Mark tells us, "They were on the road going up to Jerusalem, and Jesus was walking ahead of them; they were amazed, and those who followed were afraid" (Mark 10:32). He was not going to a party; he was going to his trial. He was not going to be crowned; he was going to be crucified. There were safer places he could have gone, but they were not the places he believed God wanted him to go. So he went on with a set face, a firm step, a resolute heart.

In 1893, Governor John P. Altgeld of Illinois extended pardon to three men who had been sentenced in connection with the Haymarket labor riots of May 4, 1886. Four others had already been executed, after trials conducted in the midst of public hysteria. Altgeld knew he would be going against public opinion to pardon the men, but he said: "If I decide they are innocent, I will pardon them if I never hold office another day."[4]

That kind of spirit is a far cry from that of the person who looks carefully down the road of some needed action and sees danger or cost there and decides to take another route. Christ's call is to travel the road of obedience to God regardless of what it may cost.

A Standard For Evaluation
To say this is to be reminded of how prone we are to avoid routes that may appear dangerous or costly. So many times our first question is not, "Is this the will of God?" It is, "What will this

14

cost, in time, in energy, in money, in prestige?" We wonder about the danger that may be involved — danger to our hopes, dreams, plans, goals. Christ is supposed to be our Example, but when we look at our disloyalty to the will of God in the light of Christ's faithfulness to that will, we have to blush in shame.

Eric Hoffer, the longshoreman philosopher, lost his eyesight when he was a child, but regained it at age fifteen. He never bothered to find out why he became blind or how his sight was restored. Expecting to die before he was fifty, since most Hoffer family members did, he spent ten years of his life as a tramp or hobo. He later wrote, "I went through life like a tourist."[5]

If you go through life "like a tourist," you can avoid a lot of decisions about the direction in which to set your face. That is drifting, without aim or purpose, but it is no longer discipleship to Jesus Christ. Christ is always the Man with the set face. At whatever point we observe him, we see him moving intentionally, purposefully. And he keeps calling us, too, to deliberate living, intentional choosing of the direction our lives are to take.

But our choices must not cater to our selfishness, or feed our prejudices, or give vent to our resentments. Our determination must not be mere stubbornness or spite or vindictiveness. Our faces must be set on the basis of something other than ambition or greed or lust or pride or the desire for a good time.

Christ's set face is the standard and guide for us. He said once, "My food is to do the will of him who sent me and to complete his work" (John 4:34). He lived to do God's will, and when he died it was in the way of obedience to that will. That must be our standard and goal, too. That will not always be easy, but as we seek to do it, we will experience our fullest development, find our truest fulfillment, and realize our greatest usefulness.

It may be that a frequent glance at the Christ with the set face will help to keep us aroused to our responsibilities, committed to the purposes that ought to possess us, and devoted to the God who made and loves us.

1. Leo Tolstoy, *War and Peace*, Great Books of the Western World edition (Chicago: Encyclopedia Britannica, Inc., 1952), Vol. 51, p. 665.

2. Paul Tillich, *My Travel Diary*, edited by Jerald C. Brauer (New York, Evanston, and London: Harper & Row, Publishers, 1970), p. 119.

3. Edwin Charles Dargan, *A History of Preaching* (New York: Hodder & Stoughton and George H. Doran Company, 1905), Vol. I, pp. 484-486.

4. Harry Golden, *Carl Sandburg* (Greenwich, Connecticut: Fawcett Publications, Inc., 1961), p. 52.

5. Eric Hoffer, *Truth Imagined* (New York: Harper & Row, Publishers, 1983), p. 2.

2.

The Wasted Ointment

Matthew 26:6-13; Mark 14:3-9; Luke 7:36-50; John 12:1-8

*"Now while Jesus was at Bethany in the house of Simon the leper,
a woman came to him with an alabaster jar of very costly ointment, and she poured it on his head as he sat at the table."*

— Matthew 26:6

One of Abraham Lincoln's most famous speeches was his
"House Divided" speech in which he declared that the nation could
not continue forever half slave and half free. Because of that speech,
he was called a radical and an agitator and other uncomplimentary
names. Even his friends thought he had gone too far. But he said:
"If I had to draw a pen across my record and erase my whole life
from sight, and I had one poor gift or choice left as to what I should
save from the wreck, I should choose that speech and leave it to
the world unerased."[1]

If that choice were yours in regard to the record of your life,
what would you leave to the world unerased? There may be plenty
you would like to blot out, but what, above all else, would you
want to leave unerased?

Jesus made a prediction once about something one person did
that would make her immortal in history. She herself had no idea
she was acting for posterity. It was not to be remembered that she
did what she did. She had other motives than that. But Jesus said
about her deed, "Truly, I say to you, wherever this good news is
proclaimed in the whole world, what she has done will be told in
remembrance of her" (Matthew 26:13).

17

Jesus' own disciples, however, did not value her deed that highly. In fact, it seemed to them a foolish, wasteful act. In an extravagant expression of affection, this woman had come bursting into the home of Simon of Bethany where Jesus and his disciples were guests at a meal, and had poured an alabaster jar of expensive ointment on Jesus' head (the Gospels of Luke and John say she anointed Jesus' feet). The cost of the ointment represented nearly a year's wages for the average laborer. Transferred back into money, the ointment could have put bread in the mouths of hungry children and clothes on their backs. But it couldn't now; it was gone, poured out in an instant, never to be recovered again. The disciples were indignant at such waste.

But Jesus reacted differently. He reproved his disciples for their criticism of the woman. He saw beauty in her act, and predicted that her extravagant deed of love would be known in all ages and all places where the gospel was proclaimed.

If you had been there, which side would you have taken on this? Would you have commended or condemned the woman? Would you, like the disciples, have called this ointment "wasted" ointment?

An Expression Of Self-Forgetful Love

It was a deed of beauty in Jesus' eyes, because it was an expression of self-forgetful love. There was nothing calculating about this act. The woman had nothing to gain by it. Indeed, she was not interested in gaining by it. She had already been on the gaining side (see Luke 7:47). Her life had been lifted to a new plane, filled with new meaning and purpose, infused with a new joy. And Jesus was responsible for this. She had gained enough! Now she wanted to give something. She wanted to express in a visible and tangible way the gratitude she felt. So forgetting herself and the things she might have secured with that expensive ointment, she poured it all out in a burst of affection and gratitude. And Jesus did not miss the beauty of what she did.

Do you know O. Henry's beautiful story about a young couple just getting started in their lives together? It is Christmas time and they have no money to buy gifts for each other. The young wife's most precious possession is her long, beautiful hair, and on a sudden impulse on Christmas Eve, she sells her hair for $20 to get money for a present for her husband. His most treasured possession is a lovely watch, and she finds a splendid platinum fob chain and purchases it as his gift. In the meantime, he too is shopping. He knows she has often looked longingly at some expensive combs in a store window. They are pure tortoise shell, with jeweled rims, just the shade to wear in her beautiful hair. He buys them as her Christmas gift, but to get the money for the purchase, he has to sell his cherished watch. Each then is unable to use the gift the other gives, but it doesn't matter, for they know the joy of self-forgetful love.[2]

So often what we do is calculated to benefit us in some way. We place such a high value on our own welfare, our own interests, our own desires, and the result is one calculated act after another. There is little beauty in that kind of living; it has no claim to commendation. But every now and then some person pours out the "alabaster jar" of self in the interests of another, and his or her life takes on a beauty it has not shown before.

That's why Jesus commended this woman! She was acting in love, uninterested in gain for herself. She was pouring out, not just expensive ointment, but selfless devotion and gratitude as well.

A Defiance Of The Market Mind

The thing that bothered the disciples about this was that they saw no value in it. The woman was giving expression to her feelings, but what good could come from that? What kind of return could be expected from poured-out ointment? It just didn't pay to waste expensive products like that.

But their trouble was that they were possessed by the "market mind." The market mind is concerned about dollars and cents. It is interested in sales and profits. It has no tolerance for waste. Everything must pay. If it doesn't, it must be stopped.

The market mind has its place. Its importance must not be discounted. Commerce would not function without it. It is due the credit for numerous good things in our society. But Jesus, in his rebuke of the market mind on this occasion, was saying that there are times when the principle of the marketplace just does not apply.

This is true, for one thing, because we are not mere flesh and blood, but mind and spirit, too. So it is not enough to be concerned only about the most obvious needs. One can be well-fed and yet be starving. One can be warmly clothed and still be cold. One can be surrounded by people and yet feel lonely. One can have everything money can buy and still be miserably impoverished so far as meaning and purpose and joy are concerned.

In other words, it is essential to look for a different kind of dividend than the market mind ordinarily expects. And sometimes what appear to be useless and even wasteful actions can contribute to the creating of that dividend.

Another reason why the principle of the marketplace does not always apply is that it is too easy to be short-sighted. Then one thinks something has no value if it does not immediately produce the effects one desires. In addition to the possibility that one may be looking for the wrong kind of effects, one may also be in too big a hurry to see them.

On the surface, for instance, it may seem wasteful to invest money in a church building, and worship may seem irrelevant in the face of the desperate cries of a needy world. But who can measure the influence of that building and what takes place inside it and because of it? Who knows how much meaning is given, how much purpose is created, how much comfort is imparted, how much courage is inspired, how much generosity is motivated, how much love is expressed because of what takes place there?

The market mind has its place, but that wasted ointment defies its tendency to pervade every area of society and every aspect of life.

A Testimony To Arrested Opportunity

It is also a testimony to arrested opportunity. Some might call it a reminder of the permanence of poverty. "You always have the poor with you," Jesus said (Matthew 26:11). The disciples were more than a bit impertinent to be reminding him of the poor. He knew about them, and he never intended that anything he said

20

should make their needs seem less pressing to others. In one of his parables, he even made the way one responded to the needs of others the basis of final judgment (Matthew 25:31-46).

But when he said, "You always have the poor with you," it was not the perpetuity of poverty that was uppermost in his mind. It was his own brief remaining time with his disciples. "You will not always have me," he said (Matthew 26:11). Here they were, mouthing a pious platitude when they could have been doing something to lighten the heavy load he was bearing. Soon the opportunity to do that would be gone, and it would not come again. But there was one person who did not let this opportunity slip by, and that wasted ointment is witness to that fact.

Saturday Review once carried a cartoon showing a knight in full armor riding his horse toward the desert and past a sign that read, "Leaving populated area ... Last chance to do a chivalrous act."[3] This was perhaps this woman's last chance to shower Jesus with love and gratitude, and she was not letting that chance glide by. She was arresting it, stopping it.

The only way to arrest an opportunity is to seize it. If it is not touched, it passes on; if it is not used, it fades away, and what it offered is lost.

Van Wyck Brooks wrote once, "My political creed is based on the assumption that everybody ought to be given a chance. My literary creed is based on the assumption that few will ever take the chance."[4] This woman's wasted ointment testifies to the fact that she took the chance; she showed her love and gratitude for the One who had so immeasurably enriched her life.

A Call To Devoted Action

When you look at her deed in a rational way, it is not too impressive. Its physical effects could not have lasted very long. But it meant something to Jesus that could not be explained in terms alone of the outward actions and elements involved in it.

He was living at that time in the shadow of the cross. He was already feeling the sting of his rejection by the world. He knew his disciples well enough to know that even they, his closest friends, would desert him when the going got toughest. Perhaps what he needed then more than anything else was the fellowship of those who loved him. So he was strengthened by this woman's extravagant and unrestrained expression of affection and gratitude. Not much could be done for him, but what she could do, she did, and Jesus was pleased. He said, "She has done what she could" (Mark 14:8).

Christ is always pleased when one does what one can. For many of us, that is an unexciting and unspectacular thing to do. We'd like to do something else. Something else would be so much more interesting and useful. But that poured out ointment should encourage us to do what we can instead of complaining of how little we can do or waiting for an opportunity to do something big and significant.

The world owes most, not to those who sought to do great things, but to those who were faithful in little things. The truly useful people are the ones who devote themselves to doing what they can even when it is not what they would like to be doing.

Waste has been characteristic of modern American society. Yet we, too, think it strange that a person should become immortal in history for an act of wastefulness. But this was only because Jesus saw the true nature and value of her deed and called it a thing of beauty. He knew her deed was a defiance of the market mind that thinks primarily in terms of dollars and cents. He knew she was arresting an opportunity that would not be hers again, and was doing the little she could do to ease his own hurt and sorrow. And he saw that she was doing it out of gratitude and self-forgetful love.

It is not for waste that we should desire to be remembered or to receive Christ's commendation. But it may be that if the kind of outlook and desire that motivated that woman long ago could possess us, we too might have the thrilling experience of hearing Christ say of us that we have "done a beautiful thing to (him)" (Matthew 26:10 RSV).

---

1. Carl Sandburg, *Abraham Lincoln* (New York: Charles Scribner's Sons, 1925, 1926), Vol. II, p. 106.

2. O. Henry, "The Gift of the Magi," in *Great Short Stories* (New York: Award Books, Inc., n.d.), pp. 14-18.

3. *Saturday Review*, October 9, 1971, p. 27.

4. Van Wyck Brooks, *From a Writer's Notebook* (New York: E.P. Dutton and Co., Inc., 1958), p. 129.

3.

The Pointing Table

Matthew 26:17-30; Mark 14:12-26; Luke 22:7-28

"When the hour came, he took his place at the table, and the apostles with him." — Luke 22:14

Part of Jesus' last night with his disciples was spent gathered around a table. To say that this was a table that pointed is to say what, in a physical sense, could be said about any table — unless it were round or some other shape, of course. But it is not in a physical sense that I am thinking now. True, the table pointed physically, but it pointed also in a far more significant sense than that. Let's say, to begin with, that it pointed to events.

The thoughts of Jesus and the disciples as they reclined around that table were not of the table itself. Yet the table had a part in their thinking; we might say that it was an aid to thought, and the table itself is forever associated with what was said and done there that night.

The table pointed in two directions: It pointed to the past, and it pointed to the future. At least as Jesus used the table, that was what it did. What took place around that table pointed the thoughts of his disciples both toward the past and toward the future.

To A Deliverance

First, the table pointed to the past. Scholars are not agreed as to whether or not this was the Passover meal that Jesus was eating with his disciples. The truth is that the Gospels themselves do not agree about that. The Gospels of Matthew, Mark, and Luke — the so-called Synoptic Gospels — indicate that it was, and the Gospel

25

of John implies that it was not. But at any rate, it was the Passover season, and it is not likely that a special meal like this could have been eaten without the thoughts of the participants turning back to that Passover in Egypt centuries before. The table around which they reclined pointed them to that momentous event in the distant past.

The Hebrews considered this event so significant that they felt themselves under obligation to recall it again and again. They had been delivered from the misery of Egyptian slavery in so dramatic a fashion that they could not but believe that it was God who had delivered them. They needed to remember this; so once a year they had a special meal in which they commemorated that deliverance.

It was a time of remembering, of reliving the experiences through which their forebears had passed. It was a time of thanksgiving, of expressing gratitude for their deliverance and for God's watchful care through the centuries. And it was also a time when the participants in the meal committed themselves anew to loyalty and obedience to the God to whom they owed so much.

We have no reason for doubting that Jesus regularly kept the Passover. He was not bound by tradition, it is true, yet he pushed aside only the traditions that were a hindrance to the true service of God. So he must have been glad for the table at which he had his last meal with his disciples to point them to that event whose remembering would help them to be truer to God. Indeed, he must even have wanted the table so to point them.

To A Cross

It was not the distant past, however, that was uppermost in Jesus' mind during that meal. They were eating in the shadow of a cross, and what he said and did there caused that table to point to that cross also.

In his *Letters from the Earth*, Mark Twain, telling the story of Adam and Eve in the Garden, says that God warned them that they would die if they ate the forbidden fruit. That was a strange thing for God to say, Twain says, "for the reason that inasmuch as they had never seen a sample of death they could not possibly know what he meant."[1]

26

But Jesus' disciples had seen samples of it, maybe even samples caused by crosses, and they knew that "Death is a grim dividing door / That shuts and keeps its tenants fast."[2]

Jesus might then have done what is commonly done today: He might have avoided the subject of death. That was not a pleasant subject at all; why discuss it? A meal with one's friends — especially a last meal — should not be ruined by thoughts of death!

But James Baldwin says that "perhaps the whole root of our trouble, the human trouble, is that we will sacrifice all the beauty of our lives, will imprison ourselves in totems, taboos, crosses, blood sacrifices, steeples, mosques, races, armies, flags, nations, in order to deny the fact of death, which is the only fact we have."[3]

Jesus, however, was not denying or ignoring the fact of death. He was facing and accepting it, and he wanted his disciples to do the same. He was not interested though just in their getting used to the idea of death, like Aldous Huxley wrote about in *Brave New World*. Huxley described a world in which freedom was dead and all concepts of morality were forgotten. Savage, this left-over from a previous and inferior civilization, is being shown around this brave new world, and he sees five busloads of boys and girls roll past over the vitrified highway. Dr. Gaffney, the Provost at the school Savage is visiting, explains: "Just returned from the Slough Crematorium. Death conditioning begins at eighteen months. Every tot spends two mornings a week in a Hospital for the Dying. All the best toys are kept there, and they get chocolate cream on death days. They begin to take dying as a matter of course."[4]

It was not "death conditioning" Jesus was seeking for his disciples as they ate and talked together that night. He was not afraid of death; he knew there were greater dangers than dying. But if there was anything he did not want, it was for his disciples to take his dying as a matter of course. He wanted them to remember it, and so he called it specifically to their attention, gave them symbols of it, and told them to let those symbols keep reminding them of his death.

This is really a remarkable thing. He spoke many profound and significant words and performed numerous beautiful and meaningful deeds. But, as Alexander Maclaren said, "The moment in which he gave his life is what he would imprint forever on the memory of the world."[5]

Certainly, this was not because death is a lovely thing, nor because it is a tragic thing. He wanted them to remember his death because it is an instrument of the salvation of God. Multitudes, remembering his death, have found themselves being reconciled to God and brought into a saving relationship with God.

No wonder Jesus wanted that table in the upper room to point to a cross, and no wonder either that he wants us to gather again and again at a table which points, nearly twenty centuries later, back to that cross and to his death on it.

To A Kingdom

There is a story that when Ben Hecht was a reporter for the Chicago *Daily News* and sent in bloody preliminary details about a hanging, the editor, Henry Justin Smith, sent word saying: "Please omit gruesome details. Remember ours is a family newspaper." Hecht replied, "Will make hanging cheerful as possible."[6]

It is not possible to make a hanging very cheerful. Yet when the early Christians gathered at what they called "The Lord's Table," they did so with great joy, though that table pointed them back to an ugly crucifixion. Jesus himself inserts a note of joyful anticipation in his conversation with his disciples. All was not gloom and despair there, for Jesus did not believe that his death would put an end to the purposes of God. In a little while he would be surrounded by men with staves and spears; he would be condemned and executed as a criminal, but God would not be defeated. God's kingdom would be culminated yet.

So Jesus talked about drinking the fruit of the vine with his disciples again, but this time in his Father's kingdom. He said, "I tell you, I will never again drink of this fruit of the vine until that day when I drink it new with you in my Father's kingdom" (Matthew 26:29). MacLean Gilmore says that for Jesus that supper was a "feast of anticipation," for Jesus looked beyond the cross and the grave to a victory wicked men could not prevent.[7]

He knew that dark moments were ahead for these dear friends, but he wanted them to know that there would be other moments

28

and another day. T. S. Eliot expresses something of Christ's faith when he has Archbishop Thomas Becket, with death imminent before him, to say that another moment is coming "when the figure of God's purpose is made complete."[8]

"The figure of God's purpose!" Jesus believed that God's purpose included but extended beyond the dark hours in which they were then living. So he did not talk simply about his death, but also about the coming kingdom and the gladness they would know together then. He himself had, and he wanted his disciples also to have, a quality of faith that would keep them looking forward to the coming kingdom, even in the midst of the tragedy of the cross.

He wants us to have that same faith today. It is not hard to become pessimistic about humankind and our world, but Christ calls us to the faith that says, with Tennyson:

> Our little systems have their day,
> They have their day and cease to be;
> They are but broken lights of thee,
> And thou, O Lord, art more than they.[9]

Christ is more than "our little systems" and more than we ourselves; so we can believe that God is not through with us or our world yet, and we can trust that someday we will know that "The kingdom of the world has become the kingdom of our Lord and of his Messiah, and he will reign forever and ever" (Revelation 11:15).

"When the hour came, he took his place at the table, and the apostles with him." There was nothing distinctive about the appearance of that table, but what was said and done around it that night has caused so many other tables to be called "The Lord's Table." It was a table that pointed — to the past and to the future. And all of the Tables of the Lord today point, too. They point to the past, to a cross and a dying Savior, and they point also to the future, giving us sound basis for hope in the consummation and perfecting of the Kingdom of our Lord.

1. Mark Twain, *Letters from the Earth* (Greenwich, Connecticut: Fawcett Publications, Inc., Crest Reprint, 1963), p. 578.

2. John Masefield, "The Night of Kings," in *The Bluebells and Other Verse* (New York: The Macmillan Co., 1961), p. 22.

3. James Baldwin, *The Fire Next Time* (New York: Dial Press, 1963), p. 105.

4. Aldous Huxley, *Brave New World* (New York: Bantam Books, 1953), p. 110.

5. Alexander Maclaren, *Expositions of Holy Scripture, Matthew 18-28* (New York: A. C. Armstrong and Son; London: Hodder and Stoughton, 1906), p. 244.

6. Harry Golden, *Carl Sandburg* (Greenwich, Connecticut: Fawcett Publications, Inc., Crest Reprint, 1961), p. 161.

7. S. MacLean Gilmore, Exegesis of Luke in *The Interpreter's Bible* (Nashville: Abingdon Press, 1952), Vol. VIII, p. 377.

8. T. S. Eliot, "Murder in the Cathedral," in *The Complete Poems and Plays* (New York: Harcourt, Brace & World, Inc., 1962), p. 209.

9. Alfred Lord Tennyson, "In Memoriam."

4.

The Saving Prayer

Matthew 26:31-35; Mark 14:26-31; Luke 22:31-34

"Simon, Simon, listen! Satan has demanded to sift all of you like wheat, but I have prayed for you that your own faith may not fail; and you, when once you have turned back, strengthen your brothers."
— Luke 22:31-32"

Once during Dietrich Bonhoeffer's pastorate in London in the 1930s, he was told that certain Roman Catholic congregations prayed for the imprisoned and persecuted members of the German Confessing Church. When some of his colleagues indicated that they saw nothing remarkable in that, Bonhoeffer reacted sharply, saying: "I am not indifferent to somebody praying for me."[1]

Simon Peter had been among those — he might even have been their spokesman — who came to Jesus at the conclusion of one of his periods of prayer and said, "Lord, teach us to pray" (Luke 11:1). He had been witness to the effects of Jesus' praying in Jesus' own life and also in the lives of others. Can you imagine him then being indifferent when Jesus looked him in the eye and said, "I have prayed for you"?

Paul wrote that "we do not know how to pray as we ought" (Romans 8:26), but I doubt that Peter would have thought that applied to Jesus. Jesus knew human nature well enough to be acquainted with the common, universal needs of persons. The purposes of God were clear enough to him to give direction to his praying. His own motives were so pure that his attitudes and purposes would never stand in the way of his prayers. And then he knew Peter like a book. Is it likely at all that Peter would have been unmoved by the knowledge that his Lord had prayed for him?

Prayed With Awareness Of Danger

Jesus' prayer was prayed with awareness of the danger in which Peter stood. He said, "Satan has demanded to sift all of you like wheat." These words, as the *New Revised Standard Version* makes clear, were meant for all the disciples, for the Greek word for "you" in this statement is plural. It is as if Jesus were reminding his closest friends that he is not the only one contending for their allegiance. The danger they confront is imminent and serious, and it makes a difference whether they escape from it or succumb to it.

Svetlana Alliluyeva, daughter of Joseph Stalin, was writing about her Aunt Anna and said: "She was endowed in highest measure with the trustfulness and simplicity of spirit of the truly honorable person, one who is incapable of suspecting anyone else of wrongdoing because he is incapable of it himself."[2]

Why would Jesus, pure and honorable as he was, suspect that his disciples would be guilty of a wrongdoing of which he himself was incapable? Maybe it was because, though he was the purest and best of persons, he was a realist, too, and so refused to ignore the fact of the universality of temptation and its perpetual nature. That picture in the opening chapter of the Book of Job could very well have been in his mind. It is a scene in the heavenly court when "the heavenly beings came to present themselves before the Lord, and Satan also came among them. The Lord said to Satan, 'Where have you come from?' Satan answered the Lord, 'From going to and fro on the earth, and from walking up and down on it' " (Job 1:6-7). Satan never stays still; he is never off the job!

It might have seemed to some that night that the kind of danger Jesus had in mind was far removed from these dear friends of his. It was obvious enough to them, a little later, that others might betray their Lord, or deny him, or take other courses in completely opposite directions from those which allegiance to Christ would require. But they were his friends. They loved him; they had bound themselves to him with the ties of love and loyalty. They were in no danger of breaking those bonds.

But Jesus knew in his own experience the power of the Evil One who was always "going to and fro on the earth, and ... walking up and down on it." Jesus had had his own encounters with the Devil, and he knew only too well the danger in which Peter and the other disciples stood.

After Jesus' struggle with Satan and his victory over him at the beginning of his public ministry, Luke tells us that "when the devil had finished every test, he departed from him until an opportune time" (Luke 4:13). It was not a surrender on Satan's part; it was only a temporary truce, an interlude during which Satan would look for further opportunities to work havoc in Jesus' heart and life. That, Jesus knew, was what his disciples, too, could expect from the Tempter.

After Francis Asbury had been a bishop in early American Methodism for 22 years, he wrote to one of his preachers, "I have only to say I sit on a joyless height, a pinnacle of power too high to sit secure and unenvied, too high to sit secure without divine aid."[3]

Whether one's station is high or low in the eyes of people, one cannot sit secure without divine aid. Christ looks upon us, too, with awareness of the spiritual danger confronting us.

Prayed With Confidence In Peter's Future

Yet Jesus' prayer for Peter was prayed with confidence in Peter's future. He did not ignore the probability of Peter's falling, but he denied that that was the end for him. He prayed that his faith might not fail — that is, that his fall might not be permanent or ruinous, but that his dreadful sin might be followed by genuine penitence. And in anticipation of his prayer being answered, he gave Peter a commission: "When once you have turned back, strengthen your brothers."

Jesus wanted Peter to know that his denial of him did not have to be the end of either his faith or his usefulness. His faith might go into eclipse, but it did not have to be extinguished. He might be momentarily unfaithful to his deepest convictions, but his convictions did not have to be annihilated by his unfaithfulness.

I would not minimize the seriousness of any denial of Christ or any unfaithfulness to God. The Cross speaks too clearly for

33

that. But if the gospel means anything at all, it means hope for persons who have failed or fallen. It speaks of new prospects and new beginnings. It does not take lightly the damage our sins may do to us or to others, but it says that new life may spring forth where there seemed to be only death.

Dr. Paul Tournier says that "in this world, our task is not so much to avoid mistakes, as to be fruitful." He affirms the importance of increasing in ability to recognize our faults, so that we may better understand God's mercy. But he warns against becoming obsessed with our faults. He says, "Our vocation is, I believe, to build good out of evil. For if we try to build good out of good, we are in danger of running out of raw material."[4]

A little later that night, Peter must have thought that he had "run out of raw material." But Jesus had prayed for him, and by God's grace he found in his experience of failure and sin materials he was able to use to build a beautiful and tremendously useful life.

Many years ago, I heard Bishop F. Gerald Ensley preach a sermon at Lake Junaluska, North Carolina, on the topic, "Making Our Sins Useful." What a practical topic! There is a place for emphasis on avoiding sins, but it is also appropriate to think about how we can take our broken vows, our confused priorities, our cowardly denials, our impulsive mistakes, our errors of judgment, and make them into building blocks for a life of beauty and usefulness. Bishop Ensley said that our sins can do three things for us: They can inspire us to amend our lives; they can instruct us in what not to do; and they can give us an entrée to help others. It is interesting that that last is what Jesus specified for Peter: He told him to strengthen his brothers. He gave a commission to a person who was about to fail. He wanted him to know that he had a future in stability and virtue and usefulness.

A few hours after Peter had passionately pledged his loyalty to Christ, he denied that he had ever even known him. Then Jesus was led by his captors near where Peter stood, and Jesus looked at Peter and their eyes met for a brief moment. Luke says that Peter remembered that Jesus had warned him that he would deny him, and "he went out and wept bitterly" (Luke 22:62). Must he not also have remembered that Jesus had prayed for him? He had been wrapped round with his Master's prayers, and so did not utterly despair but found new hope and new life.

Margery Wilson, author, actress, and lecturer of an earlier day, tells of a time coming when she first fully realized "that on this earth every perfection was somewhere marred, every brow bore some kind of scar. The trail of the serpent cut across all human effort."[5]

Peter knew something about "the trail of the serpent." He knew something about the marring of perfection, the scarring of sin. But he knew also that his Lord had prayed for him, and had told him to strengthen his brothers. Do you see the significance of Jesus' conversation with Peter by the Sea of Galilee after the Resurrection? He was talking with one who had denied that he even knew him, but Jesus said to him repeatedly, "Feed my lambs; feed my sheep" (John 21:15-19). He had denied his Lord, but Christ still had work for him to do!

We may not understand clearly what the Apostle Paul means when he talks about the Spirit interceding for us and Christ interceding for us (Romans 8:26, 34). But the important thing is for us to realize and believe that God's concern and care are not obliterated by our sins. Even when we deny Christ, he remains on the scene of our lives, reaching out to us and seeking to enable us to "build good out of evil." So, though our hearts may be marred and scarred and imperfection and failure may seem all too characteristic of our efforts and deeds, because we are wrapped round with Christ's prayers — offered in everlasting concern and love — we may hope for forgiveness, for new beginnings, for new strength, for new usefulness.

---

1. Wolf-Dieter Zimmermann and Ronald Gregor Smith, editors, *I Knew Dietrich Bonhoeffer* (New York and Evanston: Harper & Row, Publishers, 1966), p. 96.

2. Svetlana Alliluyeva, *Twenty Letters to a Friend* (New York: Avon Books, Discus Edition, 1967, 1968), p. 71.

3. J. Manning Potts, Elmer T. Clark, and Jacob S. Payton, editors, *The Journal and Letters of Francis Asbury* (London: Epworth Press; Nashville: Abingdon Press, 1958), Vol. III, p. 356.

4. Paul Tournier, *The Person Reborn* (New York, Evanston, and London: Harper & Row, Publishers, 1966), p. 80.

5. Margery Wilson, *I Found My Way* (Philadelphia and New York: J. B. Lippincott Company, 1956), p. 109.

5.

The Unwanted Cup

Matthew 26:36-46; Mark 14:32-42; Luke 22:39-46

"My Father, if it is possible, let this cup pass from me; yet not what I want but what you want."   — Matthew 26:39

On the western slopes of the Mount of Olives, just outside Jerusalem, may be seen the lovely Basilica of Gethsemane. It is built mainly of pink limestone and has a beautiful Byzantine style façade and twelve domes. Each dome is the gift of a particular country, and so the church is also called the Church of All Nations. The floor inside is paved with mosaics, and when one looks up at the twelve cupolas, one sees mosaics there, too. But one's attention is inevitably drawn toward the altar and a large rock before the altar that is enclosed by railing. This is the "Rock of Agony," so named because of the agony Jesus experienced there on the night before his crucifixion.

It was a few sleepy disciples who witnessed this agony. The whole group had retired to this place after their meal together. No doubt they had come here to sleep, but on this night something besides sleep was on Jesus' mind. All of the disciples could sense that he was troubled, but three of them, Peter and James and John, had special reason to know that he was troubled. Taking them on beyond the rest of the group, Jesus confided to them: "I am deeply grieved, even to death; remain here, and stay awake with me." They stayed there, but they did not watch for long. They were soon deep in sleep, but not before they had heard Jesus cry out, "My Father, if it is possible, let this cup pass from me; yet not what I want but what you want."

37

We don't know how long Jesus continued in prayer; we do know that he kept returning to his sleeping disciples and waking them. It was a lonely time for him, and he wanted the supporting fellowship of these, his closest friends. He did not have it though, and he had to bear his agony alone.

It was a certain "cup" that caused his agony. This "cup," of course, was not a piece of table setting. It was an especially difficult and painful experience, one Jesus desperately wanted to avoid. So it was an unwanted, unwelcome cup.

Resulting In A Cry

Jesus told his disciples to wait while he went a little farther into the garden to pray. Was this when he prayed for Peter? Not so far as we are told. The Gospel of John records what is sometimes called Jesus' "great high priestly prayer," with its setting apparently in the upper room where he had his last meal with his disciples. These disciples were uppermost in his thoughts in this prayer. He lifted them up before God, asking his Heavenly Father to guard them, to "protect them from the evil one," to "sanctify them in the truth," and to make his joy complete in them (John 17).

But his prayer in the Garden of Gethsemane, at least so far as we know, was little more than a cry: "My Father, if it is possible, let this cup pass from me." I wonder if he was having the kind of experience Paul writes about when he says that when praying is too hard for us, the "Spirit intercedes for us with sighs too deep for words" (Romans 8:26). The whole world was bearing down upon Jesus that night, but about all he could say was, "O God, O God."

Cardinal Joseph Louis Bernardin was writing about his struggle with pancreatic cancer. He told of being in the hospital and wanting to pray but finding his physical discomfort so overwhelming that he couldn't pray. He said to friends who visited him, "Pray while you're well, because if you wait until you're sick you might not be able to do it." When they looked at him in astonishment, he said, "I'm in so much discomfort that I can't focus on prayer. My faith is still present. There is nothing wrong with my faith, but in terms of prayer, I'm just too preoccupied with the pain." During his remaining months of life, he told priests and parishioners to develop a strong prayer life in their best moments so they could be sustained in their weakest moments.[1]

Was that what was happening with Jesus there in the Garden of Gethsemane? Luke tells us "an angel from heaven appeared to him and gave him strength." But Luke also says that "in his anguish he prayed more earnestly, and his sweat became like great drops of blood falling down on the ground" (Luke 22:43-44). Tell me that prayer is always a peaceful experience! What a struggle it was for Jesus that night! That unwanted cup led to a cry of anguish.

Encouraging Petitionary Prayer

Yet Jesus' prayer in the Garden of Gethsemane, cry though it was, is an encouragement to petitionary prayer. It is a contradiction of the view that the prayer of communion is the only appropriate prayer. That was not the only prayer Jesus prayed. Here in the shadow of the cross we see him petitioning God, asking God for something: "My Father, if it is possible, let this cup pass from me."

When Miss Layona Glenn went to Brazil as a missionary in 1894, she did not know the Portuguese language at all, but she determined to learn it as soon as she could. One day not long after she arrived there, a little English-speaking girl asked her if she could say the Lord's Prayer in Portuguese. She had to reply, "No, not yet." Giggling mischievously, the little girl teased, "Miss Glenn don't know the Lord's Prayer in Portuguese." Another little girl immediately came up and put her arm around Miss Glenn's shoulder and said, "Don't you worry, Miss Glenn, I think the Lord understands English!"[2]

Jesus knew that God understands not only whatever language one may speak, but the cries, the very desires of one's heart as well. So one can afford to be honest with God; indeed, one cannot afford to be anything else. In all of our dealings with God, including our prayers, God expects us to be open and above-board. That means that it would be hypocritical to ban petitions from our prayers.

The prayers we offer to God ought to mean something to us. There is no question that Jesus' prayer that night was deeply felt by him; he wanted that cup to pass. But though his petition was not granted, the unwanted cup and Jesus' prayer about it should be an encouragement to us to be honest with God and to bring the true desires of our hearts before God in sincere prayer.

Unmasking Sin

The unwanted cup should also challenge the easy view of sin it is so easy to develop.

Who knows the full contents of this cup? It must have contained the loneliness of rejection, the consequence of loving in the face of hatred, the agony of a Divine plan resulting in the disaster of the cross with its torture and shame, and the dark night of submission to death, humankind's last enemy. But regardless of how one may describe that from which Christ wanted to be delivered, sin shows up in the picture. Sin was responsible for the unwanted cup, and that cup unmasks sin and shows it in its true horribleness.

It was not Christ's own sin though. Some other person might have feared the unveiling of heart that was soon to take place as one's earthly days came to an end and one stood before God for judgment. But Christ had no skeletons in his closet; he had no fear of his life lying open like a book before the eyes of the Eternal Judge.

So it was the sin of others that caused that unwanted cup. One after another the roll could be called and the sin named that contributed to Jesus' fate. In the tragedy that befell him, we see too clearly for mistaking the direction in which sin leads and the consequences that follow it.

And yet there is more than just the normal consequence of sin involved here. Jesus was not simply reaping the usual fruits of others' sins. In some way that we cannot fully comprehend, he was also taking upon himself the burden and guilt of all persons' sins. A little later, as he hung on the cross, he was to experience the final and ultimate consequence of sin and cry out, "My God, my God, why have you forsaken me?" (Matthew 27:46). Perhaps there in the Garden, he was already beginning to experience that

40

sense of desolation and separation, and it was almost more than he could bear.

To grasp the enormity of what was happening to Jesus then is to see the unmasking of sin. The cross snatches the mask off the face of sin and reveals it in its true ugliness and horridness.

Calling For Trust And Obedience

There have been and most likely will be again "unwanted cups" in the lives of most of us. They will never be of such vastness and eternal significance as the one that confronted Jesus. But he has shown us the spirit in which we are to face and to deal with them.

What did Jesus say to his Heavenly Father? "My Father, if it is possible, let this cup pass from me; yet not what I want but what you want." And again, "My Father, if this cannot pass unless I drink it, your will be done." Even in his agony, willing obedience was the dominating attitude of his soul.

There is no question that his desire for avoidance of this cup was strong, yet he never attempted to manipulate God or to bargain with God. He set no conditions for his obedience. He wanted the cup to pass, but there was something else he wanted even more: He wanted God's will to be done.

Jesus could have gone over the hill and escaped, but he chose to obey instead. This was not just helpless submission to God's will. It was not the resignation of defeat. He did not submit in bleak regret or in bitter anger. His was a willing obedience. He chose to have God's will done in his life.

And he did it in trust. That was why he was peaceful after his time of struggling with God. His confidence in God was not obliterated. He had a lifetime of trust behind him, and even in his agony he still thought of God as "Father." He was confident that God's will was the best will, and he had no fear of trusting himself to God. That kind of trust produces peace.

"My Father, if it is possible, let this cup pass from me; yet not what I want but what you want." This unwanted cup that Jesus ultimately chose to drink elicited a cry of agony from his soul. Yet for us it is an encouragement to be open and honest with God and to bring the real desires of our hearts to God. That cup unmasks

41

sin so that we should never again take our own sins or anyone else's lightly. And it calls us to the spirit of willing obedience and humble trust in God modeled so supremely by Jesus in that dark night of agony.

1. Joseph Cardinal Bernardin, *The Gift of Peace* (Chicago: Loyola Press, 1997), pp. 67-68.

2. Layona Glenn with Charlotte Hale Smith, *I Remember, I Remember* (Old Tappan, New Jersey: Fleming H. Revell Company, 1969), pp. 87-88.

6.

The Betraying Kiss

Matthew 26:47-50; Mark 14:43-46;
Luke 22:47-53; John 18:1-5

"Now the betrayer had given them a sign, saying, 'The one I will kiss is the man; arrest him.' At once he came up to Jesus and said, 'Greetings, Rabbi!' and kissed him."   — Matthew 26:48-49

On a television program prior to the 2000 presidential election, two female journalists were discussing the prospects of the primary candidates. They both agreed that if Vice President Al Gore won, "the kiss" would be one of the reasons for his victory. They were referring to his long and passionate kiss of his wife Tipper on the platform at the Democratic National Convention as he was about to make his nomination acceptance speech. The journalists said that that kiss would influence women voters because they saw love and affection for his wife in it.

I was surprised to hear people beginning so quickly to refer to that kiss as "the kiss." I thought there was another kiss far more famous — or infamous — than that one. It is older, too. In fact, it has been nearly 2,000 years since it was given — or, rather, used. The setting was vastly different; the occasion was radically dissimilar. The kiss was from one man to another, not on a brilliantly lighted platform before thousands of cheering people, but in a dark garden lighted only by lanterns and torches carried by "a large crowd with swords and clubs."

This kiss was to be an identifying kiss. Its presenter said to those with him, "The one I will kiss is the man; arrest him." He was to kiss his friend with whom he had traveled, to whose teachings he had listened, and whom he had watched perform many marvelous deeds. It helped to turn his friend over to people who were not his friends but his enemies and who wanted him removed from human society.

That, in my book, is "The Kiss!"

An Oath Of Allegiance?

In his play, *Cyrano de Bergerac*, Edmond Rostand has his hero give a beautiful definition of a kiss. Cyrano is an extremely unhandsome person in love with the beautiful Roxanne. Roxanne does not know that Cyrano loves her; she thinks she is in love with a young cadet by the name of Christian. Cyrano does not want to hurt Roxanne, and so since Christian is unable to express his love, Cyrano does it for him. He writes beautiful letters for Christian and instructs him in his courtship. Then one night while Roxanne is on the balcony of her home, Cyrano has Christian serenade her from the courtyard below. For a while he whispers to Christian what to say to her, but then suddenly he begins to speak aloud, expressing in lavish poetic language the love Cyrano himself feels for Roxanne. At the climax of the scene, he is speaking of a kiss and says:

> *"A kiss! When all is said, what is a kiss? An oath of allegiance taken in closer proximity, a promise more precise, a seal on a confession, a rose red dot upon the letter I in loving; a secret which elects the mouth for ear; an instant of eternity murmuring like a bee; a balmy communion with a flavor of flowers, a fashion of inhaling each other's heart, and of tasting, on the brink of the lips, each other's soul!"*[1]

Perhaps not many of us would or could define or describe a kiss like that, but gushy as this is, doesn't Cyrano say some things that strike home with us? "What is a kiss?" he asks, and then answers: "An oath of allegiance taken in closer proximity, a promise more precise, a seal on a confession."

A kiss should say something about love, about loyalty, about commitment to the one receiving the kiss. Was that what Judas' kiss was? It certainly was not like the kiss familiar to the Mrs.

44

Lockhorn of the comic strips. As Mr. Lockhorn is leaving for work one morning, she stands on the front steps and calls after him, "You forgot to absent-mindedly peck me good-bye."[2]

No oath of allegiance there, no promise of loyalty, no seal on a confession. Is that the kind of kiss Judas gave Jesus in the Garden of Gethsemane on that long ago night?

A Disguise For Betrayal

We know better. It was more than a token of indifference; it was a disguise for betrayal. Judas in that moment was following in the trail of other noted betrayers. The first kiss mentioned in the Bible involved deception. Jacob kissed his aged father Isaac while leading him to believe that he was his other son, Esau (Genesis 27:27). Prince Absalom was banished from the palace for five years because he murdered his brother. When he was finally allowed to return to the palace, he kissed his father David though he was plotting rebellion against him at that very time (2 Samuel 14:33). Joab, David's general, kissed Amasa, another of the generals, and stuck a sword in his stomach while doing it (2 Samuel 20:9-10).

The kiss was supposed to symbolize the giving of oneself, but these men took this lovely symbol and used it for their own selfish purposes. On their lips it was not an oath of allegiance; it was a disguise for betrayal.

That was what Judas' kiss was, too. No doubt he had often greeted and said farewell to Jesus with a kiss, though the reality might have been gone from the act for some time. Then when he came to the Garden of Gethsemane in the dark of night at the head of that motley crowd, it was clear that he no longer had any intention of giving allegiance to this Man from Nazareth. Yet he took this beautiful symbol of friendship and affection and used it as the instrument of betrayal of the best friend he ever had.

Composer Robert Schumann suffered intense mental and emotional anguish, and spent the last two years of his life in a mental institution. Just before the end, his wife visited him and found him to be only a ghost of a man. He seemed to recognize her for one brief flickering moment. He smiled at her and with great effort, because he had almost lost control of his limbs, put his arms around

45

her. She tried to shut out the memory of the fourteen years of their happiness, for they seemed like a mockery in that darkness. Then as she got up to leave, he kissed her. It was like the instinctive and trustful kiss of a little child. Later Mrs. Schumann said, "Never shall I forget that moment. I wouldn't give up that kiss for all the treasures in the world."[3]

What would Jesus have given for such a kiss from Judas that night? Judas' kiss was never something to remember but to forget, not to cherish but to mourn. Judas had used a symbol of love as a disguise for betrayal.

A Call To Integrity

Baron Friedrich von Hugel, the Roman Catholic philosopher and author (1852-1925), once said, "I kiss my daughter in order to love her, as well as because I love her."[4] We can understand the "because" part of this statement. We know that a kiss is supposed to be an expression of love. But does it also create love?

It may indeed nurture and nourish love, for to express love in sincerity is to help love to grow and expand and mature.

But that was not Judas' kiss in the Garden. He was professing allegiance while practicing betrayal. Did he not remember Jesus having said, "Not everyone who says to me, 'Lord, Lord,' will enter the kingdom of heaven, but only the one who does the will of my Father in heaven"? (Matthew 7:21). Jesus had called always for integrity, for trueness in the depths of one's being, and that kiss would not cover over the lack of this in Judas' heart.

And now, for the sake of our own souls, we need to see and to hear in Judas' kiss a call to integrity.

In his autobiography, the financier Bernard Baruch wrote in glowing terms of his father and of his influence upon him. He said that his father once gave him a photograph of himself with these words inscribed on it: "Let unswerving integrity always be your watchword."[5]

Would not Christ say the same to us? No kisses of the lips unless the heart is speaking and pledging its allegiance, no profession of loyalty unless the life is in line with the profession. Be true, let unswerving integrity always be your watchword.

But what if we fail — and who among us has not? Paul Willis, in a brief poem, acknowledges not only the fact of betrayal in the past, but the possiblity of such in the future, too, "As the cock crows on in the dawn of grace."[6]

Have we not given lip service to Christ's values, and then cherished and pursued different values? Have we not professed to love the Church and then given it only the remnants of our time and talents and money? Have we not talked about integrity but yet cut the corners off honesty and truthfulness? Have we not praised service and then sought to promote our own welfare rather than that of others?

Traitors' kisses, that's what they are! Judas is not the only one who has professed allegiance and devotion while betraying the Master.

Our only hope lies in Christ's forgiveness and help. He still calls us "Friend" as he did Judas that night, and as the great missionary and evangelist, E. Stanley Jones, said, Christ is "God's kiss upon the bloated lips of a prodigal humanity."[7] There is still hope for us in the midst of our denials and betrayals because there is redemption in Christ. His love is real, steadfast, and strong, and if we give him a chance, he will help us to learn to be faithful and true. Surely then we need to say with Charles Wesley:

> I want a principle within
> of watchful, godly fear,
> a sensibility of sin, a pain to feel it near.
> I want the first approach to feel
> of pride or wrong desire,
> to catch the wandering of my will,
> and quench the kindling fire.[8]

---

1. Edmond Rostand, *Cyrano de Bergerac* (New York: Harper and Row, 1936), pp. 137-138.

2. Hoest, "The Lockhorns," in *The Atlanta Constitution*, April 1, 1981.

3. Henry Thomas and Dana Lee Thomas, *Living Biographies of Great Composers* (New York: Garden City Publishing Co., Inc., 1940), pp. 150-151.

4. C. E. Simcox, *Understanding the Sacraments* (New York: Morehouse-Gorham Co., 1956), p. 14.

5. Bernard M. Baruch, *My Own Story* (New York: Pocket Books, Inc., Cardinal Edition, 1957, 1958), p. 171.

6. Paul Willis, "Passionate Sins," in *The Christian Century*, October 16, 1991, p. 934.

7. E. Stanley Jones, *How to Be a Transformed Person* (New York and Nashville: Abingdon-Cokesbury Press, 1951), p. 152.

8. Charles Wesley, "I Want a Principle Within," in *The United Methodist Hymnal* (Nashville: The United Methodist Publishing House, 1989), Number 410.

7.

The Insulting Bonds

Matthew 26:47-56; Mark 14:43-50; Luke 22:47-54; John 18:1-14

"So the soldiers, their officer, and the Jewish police arrested Jesus and bound him." — John 18:12

A part of Jesus' mission was "to proclaim release to the captives" (Luke 4:18), yet there came a time when he himself was made a captive. They "arrested Jesus and bound him."

Hands were required to do this, and other hands were put to different uses that night. The chief priests counted out money with their hands. Judas Iscariot held out his hands to receive that money. Peter warmed his hands at the fires of those who were disposing of Jesus. The other disciples wrung their hands in fear and desperation. Pilate washed his hands in a vain attempt to escape guilt. But Jesus' hands were bound, tied to secure him as a prisoner, to insure that he did not escape.

It is ironic that "a crowd with swords and clubs" came to arrest Jesus (Mark 14:43), and that in the darkness of the night and the loneliness of an olive grove. Jesus himself was struck by the absurdity of this. It represented a gross misunderstanding of the kind of person he was and of the purpose that guided him. Then still another indignity was added when they got out their ropes and tied his hands. They were not going to risk any attempts on his part to resist arrest or to inflict injury or to escape from them.

Such action was an affront to Jesus. He was gentle and kind, thoughtful and loving, and here they were, treating him like a common criminal. What an insult! There was nothing distinctive about

49

the appearance of those bonds, but the innocence and purity of the man they bound have made them infamous. They were insulting bonds!

The Captivity They Did Not Bring

They were intended to insure Jesus' captivity, but there was a kind of captivity they did not bring to him. For instance, they did not bring the captivity of harmful habits.

The ancient historian Plutarch, in writing about the ninth century B.C. Spartan ruler and lawgiver, Lycurgus, tells of his concern to exclude any persons or practices he felt would not be beneficial to his people. Plutarch says, "He was as careful to save his city from the infection of foreign bad habits as men usually are to prevent the introduction of a pestilence."[1] What wisdom!

In more recent times, writer F. Scott Fitzgerald had this same kind of concern for his daughter as she was growing up. In a letter to her, he acknowledged his worry about her smoking and some of her other activities. He promised her more privileges when she was a little older, but said, "I don't want them to become habits that will turn and devour you."[2]

Habits have a way of doing that, and if they are harmful habits the bondage is debilitating and destructive. But Jesus knew no such bondage as that. His hands were tied, but the bonds of harmful habit were not wrapped around his life.

Neither did he experience the captivity of enslaving attitudes, such as the prejudice that controlled some of those who plotted his capture in the Garden of Gethsemane that night. Charles Lamb, the English essayist and India House clerk, is said to have acknowledged, "I am, in plainer words, a bundle of prejudices, made up of likings and dislikings." Jesus, too, had his "likings and dislikings," but he was never guilty of "pre-judging" without regard to the true facts.

Maya Angelou says, "Prejudice is a burden which confuses the past, threatens the future, and renders the present inaccessible."[3] What if Jesus had been bound by that? But he was not. His captors bound him, but that captivity did not bring the bondage of prejudice — or hatred or fear or envy. More than a few in our day find themselves imprisoned by such spirits as these, but Jesus never did.

He never knew the bondage of crowd pressure either. He had plenty of such pressure, but he never succumbed to it. He had the strength and courage "to keep the world," in Robert Frost's words, "from hurrying and crowding him too much."[4] He was his own person, unswayed by the pressures of the crowd. He moved with purpose, independent of the push and pull of those who surrounded him.

Jesus could have taken a vote among his disciples to decide whether or not he should go to Jerusalem that last time, but he didn't. Neither did he ask them, there in the Garden of Gethsemane, if they thought he ought to slip over the Mount of Olives and away from Jerusalem. His conduct was never determined by what others might think of him. He never toned his message down in the face of conflict and opposition.

When Karl Barth was beginning his revolt against theological liberalism in the first quarter of the twentieth century, he wrote to a friend: "I read today a statement by Chr. Schrempf: whoever swims against the stream cannot do it arm in arm with others."[5] It is all right to be "arm in arm with others" when you can do it with integrity, but Jesus would not sacrifice principle for popularity nor conscience for conformity. So he was taken and bound, but he never knew the captivity of crowd pressure.

Augustine prayed to be loosed "from the chains which we made for ourselves."[6] We do tie ourselves with all kinds of chains — the chains of harmful habits and enslaving attitudes and the desire for ease and affirmation and approval of others. These are real bonds, but they were never about Jesus' life. His enemies seized him and bound him, but he was not bound by such things as these.

The Freedom They Did Not Affect

This means then that he knew a freedom those bonds could not affect.

Henri Nouwen was writing to his nephew in the Netherlands about spiritual freedom. He mentioned several persons, such as Dietrich Bonhoeffer, who had known that freedom in spite of bodily

51

imprisonment, and said: "Amid the most frightful forms of oppression and violence these people discovered within themselves a place where no one had power over them, where they were wholly free."[7] Jesus knew that kind of freedom, and it was not disturbed by the bonds that made him a prisoner.

Jesus' freedom was an inner freedom, a freedom of the spirit. This is not a freedom that is attained by shaking off all restrictions and ignoring all limitations. Real freedom is not the looseness some think it to be. To be free is not just a negative condition; it has its positive side, too. One is not simply free *from*, one is also free *for*.

Jesus was free to love; he was free to forgive; he was free to serve; he was free to respond to God, to commune with God. And the reason was that he had a kind of enslavement that freed him from all other enslavements.

C. S. Lewis wrote once about a time in his life when he had a deep-seated hatred of authority. No word in his vocabulary expressed deeper hatred than the word "interference," and he thought of Christ as the Great Interferer. He wanted some place in the innermost depth of his soul which he could surround with a barbed wire fence and guard with a "No Admittance" sign.[8] Lewis was right in seeing that a Christian can have no such place or sign. Christ himself had nothing like that in his life. God was the supreme authority in his life, and that is the kind of authority we need in our lives, too.

But the wonderful thing is that when we begin to give Christ such authority, we begin also to experience a quality of freedom that is finer than any we have ever known before. New Testament scholar John Knox said, "We are bound till he lays his strong hand on us and poor till he claims all we have."[9]

A song that was popular some years ago begins: "I wish I knew how it would feel to be free; I wish I could break all these chains holding me."[10]

Some people are chained by habits they have formed, some by attitudes they have developed, some by pressures others exert upon them. In a more positive vein, some are bound by commitments they have made or ideals they have embraced. A biographer of

President Herbert Hoover, writing about his grinding, self-lacerating labor, said: "No galley slave of old was ever more firmly riveted to his drudgery, for he was chained by his surpassing sense of duty."[11] There is much to be said for that kind of bondage, but even some of these may wonder "how it would feel to be free."

The cry for freedom is a loud cry today. It is a political cry and also a very personal cry. But unfortunately not everyone understands what genuine freedom is. Too many are interested only in being loose. The freedom Christ had in the midst of his bonds was an inner freedom, a spiritual freedom, and it came from disciplined commitment and obedience to God. He was free because of the Master he had, and those man-made bonds could not affect that freedom.

That is the freedom we need, and we will have it when Christ becomes truly the Master of our lives. Then we can sing that we know how it feels to be free, because Christ breaks "all these chains holding me."[12]

1. Plutarch, *The Lives of the Noble Grecians and Romans*, Great Books of the Western World edition (Chicago, London, Toronto, Geneva: Encyclopaedia Britannica, Inc., 1952), Vol. 14, p. 46.

2. Andrew Turnbull, editor, *F. Scott Fitzgerald: Letters to His Daughter* (New York: Charles Scribner's Sons, 1963, 1965), p. 27.

3. Maya Angelou, *All God's Children Need Traveling Shoes* (New York: Random House, Vintage Books Edition, 1986, 1987), p. 154.

4. Edward Connery Lathem, editor, *Interviews with Robert Frost* (New York, Chicago, San Francisco: Holt, Rinehart and Winston, 1966), p. 135.

5. Karl Barth and Eduard Thurneysen, *Revolutionary Theology in the Making*, translated by James D. Smart (Richmond: John Knox Press, 1964), p. 111.

6. Augustine, *The Confessions,* Great Books of the Western World edition (Chicago, London, Toronto, Geneva: Encyclopaedia Britannica, Inc., 1952), Vol. 18, p. 17.

7. Henri J. M. Nouwen, *Letters to Marc About Jesus*, translated by Hubert Hoskins (San Francisco: Harper & Row, Publishers, 1987, 1988), p. 17.

8. C. S. Lewis, *Surprised By Joy* (New York: Harcourt, Brace and Company, 1955), p. 172.

9. John Knox, *A Glory In It All* (Waco, Texas: Word Books, 1985), p. 43.

10. Billy Taylor and Dick Dallas, *I Wish I Knew How It Would Feel To Be Free*, copyright 1964 and 1968 by Duane Music, Inc.

11. Eugene Lyons, *Herbert Hoover: A Biography* (Garden City, New York: Doubleday & Company, Inc., 1964), p. 218.

12. Taylor and Dallas, *op. cit.*

8.

The Warning Dream

Matthew 27:11-26; Mark 15:1-15;
Luke 23:1-25; John 18:28—19:16

*"Have nothing to do with that innocent man, for today I have suf-
fered a great deal because of a dream about him."*
— Matthew 27:19

When all other voices were urging Pilate to crucify Jesus, one
lone voice was raised in his behalf. The religious leaders had decided to put an end to him; the crowd had turned against him;
Judas had betrayed him; Peter had denied him; the other disciples
had forsaken him. But Pilate's wife spoke for him. She said, "Have
nothing to do with that innocent man, for today I have suffered a
great deal because of a dream about him."

We don't know much about this woman. Tradition tells us that
her name was Claudia Procla, that she was interested in the Jewish
faith, and that she later became a Christian. The Greek Church has
canonized her. She has the distinction of being the only person, so
far as our records show, who spoke a word in Jesus' favor when it
seemed that the whole world was against him.

This brief appearance on the biblical stage leaves many questions about her unanswered. Indeed, many scholars question the
historicity of this event, and what we see of her here can be vari-
ously interpreted. Some would say that her message to her husband reveals only a frightened and superstitious woman, that it
tells nothing about her character or her response to Jesus. That
may be true. But since we cannot know for sure, I prefer to take a
more complimentary view than that. I choose to believe that that

55

dream was a testimony to the innocence of Jesus, that it was the response of a woman's heart to him, and that it was an effort on God's part to save Pilate.

A Testimony To The Innocence Of Jesus

Most obviously, the dream was a testimony to the innocence of Jesus. "Have nothing to do with that innocent man," she said. How Claudia had seen Jesus before is unknown to us, but here at least she was seeing him in his true character. And she now added her conviction to the feeling Pilate already had, that this was an innocent man.

In Albert Camus' novel, *The Fall*, lawyer Jean-Baptiste Clamence sees Jesus not as an innocent man but as a guilty man. That, he says, is the real reason for the terrible agony Jesus suffered. He might not have been guilty of the crime he was accused of, Camus says, but he had committed others. Clamence mentions one in particular: the Slaughter of the Innocents at the time of Jesus' birth. "Those blood-spattered soldiers, those infants cut in two filled him with horror," he says. He could never forget or cease to hear "the voice of Rachel weeping for her children," and he knew it was because of him that they had died.[1]

But who, really, would credit Jesus with guilt for this tragedy? Or perhaps we would. Haven't some of us blamed persons who were working to secure respect and justice for all for the evil done by persons who opposed their efforts? Haven't we called them "troublemakers," and felt sympathetic instead toward those who were striking out at them in prejudice and anger and hatred?

Rich, an overly ambitious young man in the play, *A Man for All Seasons*, has sold out for the sake of position. Thomas Cromwell knows what he has done and has himself been a party to it. He says to him, "It's a bad sign when people are depressed by their own good fortune." Rich denies that he is depressed. He says, "I'm lamenting. I've lost my innocence." Cromwell replies, "You lost that some time ago. If you've only just noticed it, it can't have been very important to you."[2]

Jesus never lost his innocence, but neither did he go around parading it. He did, though, ask some people one day, "Which of you convicts me of sin?" (John 8:46). Pilate was concerned about crime, not about sin, but crime he could not find in Jesus (John 18:38; 19:4; Luke 23:22). It was an innocent man who stood before him, and his wife's dream was a testimony to that innocence.

Some would say today that ours is a world where no one is completely innocent. But once there was an innocent Man. He had clean hands, a pure heart, and never lifted up his soul to what was false or swore deceitfully (Psalm 24:4). His innocence shames our guilt! Claudia's dream was a testimony to that innocence.

The Response Of A Woman's Heart To Jesus

We may see in this dream also the response of a woman's heart to Jesus.

How much Claudia knew about Jesus we do not know. She had certainly heard about him. Some of what she had heard may have come from her maids or servants. It is not impossible, of course, that she had seen him herself on the streets of Jerusalem and had heard him talk. We don't know how she felt about him, yet here in a dream we see her responding, at least in part, as many other women in Palestine did, and as millions of others across the centuries have done.

In Nathaniel Hawthorne's story, "The Birthmark," beautiful Georgiana has a crimson hand on one of her cheeks. This birthmark has become so frightful an object to her husband, Aylmer, that he has determined to perform an operation and remove the mark. He has not spoken of this intention to Georgiana, but she knows he has had a dream about it. So she questions him about the dream. In regard to its influence, Hawthorne says: "Truth often finds its way to the mind close-muffled in robes of sleep, and then speaks with uncompromising directness of matters in regard to which we practice an unconscious self-deception during our waking moments."[3]

Was this what happened in Claudia's dream? Did the response she had subconsciously wanted to make to Jesus become a conscious response in that way? We cannot be sure, but it may very well be that in this dream her womanly heart was responding to the purity and goodness and love of this strange Man of Galilee.

57

No woman's name appears in the list of the twelve disciples of Jesus, but this does not mean that there were no women among his followers. The Gospels are full of instances of women coming under the influence of Jesus and having their lives transformed by him. They even followed him to the Cross. Mark's Gospel names some of these women and says they "used to follow him and provided for him when he was in Galilee, and there were many other women who had come up with him to Jerusalem" (Mark 15:40-41).

It was the women who watched where Jesus was buried and then went to prepare spices for the anointing of his body. After the Sabbath was over, it was the women who came to his tomb and were the first to know that Christ had risen. I am not really surprised by that, for their tender hearts had responded in gratitude and love to what they had seen and felt in him.

We don't know, but let's hope that one day Claudia Procla, consciously and deliberately, made that same kind of response.

A Divine Outreach To Pilate

Consider, in the third place, that this warning dream may have been a reach of the hand of God toward Pontius Pilate.

Claudia's message to Pilate was clearly an attempt on her part to save her husband from trouble. This speaks well for her. Actually, the very fact that she was with him speaks well for her, for the wives of Roman governors did not always accompany their husbands to their assigned countries. She must have been devoted to him, and we would expect that if she felt that he was about to make a serious mistake, she would do what she could to prevent it. Her message to him was such an attempt.

But the dream itself, what about it? It would be foolish, of course, to say that all dreams are sent by God. But it would not be foolish to say that God sometimes seeks to use dreams as means of accomplishing Divine purposes. Maybe God was behind this dream of Claudia's, trying in one more way to save Pontius Pilate.

Dare we think that this would be uncharacteristic of God? Can you imagine God allowing all of the plotting and scheming against Jesus to go on without trying to intervene, not simply to prevent such an end for Jesus himself, but also to try to save Pilate and all of the others involved in those tragic activities? You see, God is a saving God, not a destroying God, and is always reaching out to lift up and to redeem.

James Weldon Johnson said: "Young man — your arm's too short to box with God."

Yet one may "box with God," and even hold God away from one's self. But that is our doing, not God's. God is not a hands-off God, but tries in more ways than we can describe or imagine to reach us all, even the worst among us with the salvation we so desperately need.

When Saint Augustine was struggling with the decision to become a Christian, he was weeping and praying in his garden one day and heard a child's voice from a neighboring house. The voice was chanting and kept repeating, "Take up and read; take up and read." Augustine was awestruck by this, for he could think of no kind of play in which children sang such words. So he took this as a command from God and, checking his tears, went to the place in the garden where he had left a volume of Paul's letters. He opened the volume and began to read, and immediately the darkness of doubt vanished away and a new peace and joy came into his heart.[4]

God's dealings with persons are not always that dramatic. Dreams, visions, or other extraordinary events are not usually the means by which God's message comes to a human heart. God may work through a set of circumstances. God's call may come through the voice of a loved one or friend. God may direct through the guidance of a teacher. A chance word that one hears, an article or book one reads, an opportunity that comes to one — these and many more may be the media of God's message, as through these God seeks to bring one to the point of commitment and obedience to God, or to new knowledge and love of God and neighbor.

We don't know, but it is far from being beyond the realm of possibility that Claudia Procla's dream was one more effort of God to reach out to Pilate and to save him.

Pilate did not heed the warning that came to him in his wife's dream. It came at a strategic moment for him, but still he did not heed it. How many of God's overtures to us are not heard or seen, and thus go unheeded?

We may not hear God's messages because they do not come in the way we expect them to come — if we expect them at all. Or we may not be sensitive enough to recognize them. But our salvation rests upon our hearing and heeding God's word to us, come however it may.

We need, then, to practice listening for God's word, and to make it the habit of our life to heed and obey.

> *Open my ears, that I may hear*
> *voices of truth thou sendest clear;*
> *and while the wave notes fall on my ear,*
> *everything false will disappear.*
> *Silently now I wait for thee,*
> *ready, my God, thy will to see.*
> *Open my ears, illumine me, Spirit divine!*[5]

1. Albert Camus, *The Fall* (New York: Alfred A. Knopf, Inc., 1956), pp. 111-113.

2. Robert Bolt, *A Man for All Seasons* (New York: Vintage Books, 1960, 1962), p. 42.

3. Nathaniel Hawthorne, *Mosses from an Old Manse.*

4. Augustine, *The Confessions*, Great Books of the Western World edition (London, Chicago, Toronto, Geneva: Encyclopaedia Britannica, Inc., 1952), Vol. 18, pp. 61-62.

5. Clara H. Scott, "Open My Eyes, That I May See," in *The United Methodist Hymnal* (Nashville: The United Methodist Publishing House, 1989), Number 454.

9.

The Useless Water

Matthew 27:11-26; Mark 15:1-15;
Luke 23:1-25; John 18:28—19:16

"So when Pilate saw that he could do nothing, but rather that a riot was beginning, he took some water and washed his hands before the crowd, saying, 'I am innocent of this man's blood; see to it yourselves.'" — Matthew 27:24

The book of Deuteronomy records an interesting provision for a rite of expiation in case of an unsolved murder. It provides that when a man is found murdered in the open country and the murderer is unknown, the elders in the nearest town are responsible for conducting a rite of expiation. A heifer that has never been used for work is to be killed in an uncultivated valley where there is running water. With priests officiating, the elders are to wash their hands over the heifer and swear: "Our hands did not shed this blood, nor were we witnesses to it." Then they are to pray: "Absolve, O Lord, your people Israel, whom you redeemed; do not let the guilt of innocent blood remain in the midst of your people Israel" (Deuteronomy 21:1-9).

Pontius Pilate was a Roman, not a Jew, but the Gospel of Matthew pictures him, too, washing his hands in ceremonial fashion. His purpose, however, is not to secure pardon for the whole community; it is to clear himself of guilt and transfer total responsibility to the Jewish people for the action being taken.

The authenticity of this story is doubted by some scholars. They say that Pilate, as a Roman government official, would not have confessed his weakness in this way before mere "colonials."

To have taken this kind of action — that is, publicly agreeing to the execution of a person whom he considered innocent — would have put him in an untenable position with the Emperor. The story is best understood, these persons say, as an attempt on the part of the Church, a generation or two after Jesus' crucifixion, to show that the Christian movement from the very beginning was recognized by Roman officials as constituting no threat to the government.

It is true that the whole story of Jesus' trial and crucifixion has often been used to feed anti-Semitism, and the Jews as a people have suffered terribly because of this. This account of Pilate's handwashing, whether authentic or not, has contributed significantly to this. But though Pilate is pictured in the Gospels as recognizing the innocence of Jesus, that does not clear him of guilt for Jesus' crucifixion. The fact that he denied his own responsibility and declared the Jews alone responsible did not make it that way.

In reality, the water he is reported to have used that day was ineffective; it was useless water. It was put to use, but it was unserviceable. There was nothing wrong with the water itself; the one using it just had unrealistic expectations of it. He expected it to do something it was incapable of doing. It could have done other things, but it did not have the needed properties to accomplish this particular purpose. At that time and place, it was simply useless, impotent water.

A Brace For Cowardice

Pilate wanted it as a brace for his cowardice. Cowardice was at least partly responsible for his not setting Jesus free. He did not really need guidance in right in this matter; he knew what was right. He simply did not have the courage to do it. The water could serve no function of encouraging and strengthening him to do what he knew he ought to do. It was put into use to brace him, to confirm him, in his cowardice.

Cowardice is not, by far, the most respectable of qualities. C. S. Lewis, in *The Screwtape Letters*, has Screwtape label cowardice as the only purely painful vice: "Horrible to anticipate, horrible to feel, horrible to remember." Screwtape is writing as the master engineer of vice, instructing junior devil Wormwood in strategies of temptation. He confesses that it is most difficult to make persons proud of their cowardice, though he has succeeded in making them proud of every other vice. He warns that, for their purposes, inducing cowardice may be detrimental, since cowardice may produce real self-knowledge and self-loathing and thus lead to repentance and humility.[1]

Conceivably this could have happened to Pilate. His cowardice could have led to self-knowledge and self-loathing and thus to repentance and humility. But he avoided that by calling in a brace for his cowardice. That water helped to chloroform his shame and to make his cowardice bearable for him.

Do not we, too, sometimes look for braces for our cowardice? When our courage wavers and we fail to do what we know we ought to do, rather than acknowledging our cowardice, do we not try to brace ourselves in it? We don't like the shame and self-loathing that come with cowardly conduct, so we have to find some way of silencing the rebuking inner voice, in order that we may be able to respect and honor ourselves.

We may say that we were misled by someone else, we may plead lack of information, physical weariness or illness, an impossible situation or something else. We don't wash our hands ceremonially as Pilate did, but our purpose is the same. We want to give the impression that we acted in good faith and with courage, rather than from unworthy motives and in cowardice.

A Plea For Wrongdoing

This in reality then becomes a plea for, a justification of, wrongdoing. Pilate intended the washing of his hands to justify his action in having Jesus crucified. He knew that Jesus should be set free, but he did not have the courage to do that. He wanted, however, to be able to say, "I am doing what is right." So he washed his hands as a plea for the rightness of his conduct.

Socrates, at his trial, said that the difficulty was "not to avoid death, but to avoid unrighteousness; for that runs faster than death." He acknowledged that he was old and moved slowly and that the slower runner, death, had overtaken him. But it was because the faster runner, unrighteousness, had overtaken his accusers.[2]

Jewish novelist Igal Mossinsohn, in a novel about Judas Iscariot, has Judas living under an assumed identity on a Mediterranean island. One day a friend by the name of Andigones brings him some scrolls containing strange tales from the land of Judea. The stories are about the betrayal, trial, and crucifixion of Jesus. Andigones thinks it particularly strange and unusual that Jesus would not defend himself and that a Roman official would pronounce a death sentence and at the same time wash his hands proclaiming himself innocent of a doomed man's blood. Judas muses to himself: he knows these Pilates, these pleasure seekers. "They do not wash their hands every time they sentence a man to death. If they did, there would be no water left in the Roman settlements."[3]

But according to the Gospel of Matthew, in this instance a Roman official did want to appear innocent. He was condemning an innocent man to death, but he wanted to do it without guilt of wrongdoing for himself. In general, he may have been unconcerned about unrighteousness overtaking him, but he did not want to be guilty of this man's death.

Do we not feel similarly about our wrongdoing? If we do wrong, we want to seem justified in so doing. We cannot bear the self-reproach, the loss of self-esteem, that results from knowing that we have been guilty of doing wrong. That is why we seek excuses for our conduct. We may do wrong, but we want to wash our hands and be able to say, "I did the right."

There is a way to do that and to do it with honesty and truth. It is the way of actuality, of really doing what one believes to be right. At times we may need to recognize and to confess that what we honestly thought was right was not right. But we must be careful that we make no plea for wrongdoing, that we never seek to wash our hands of responsibility for wrongs we have done. Rather, we must seek, in honesty, to be guided by what we truly believe to be right.

A Means Of Self-Deception

Even then it is difficult to avoid self-deception. It is altogether possible that Pilate did not avoid it. He may very well have gone from his judgment hall with the feeling that he was not responsible for the sentence he had pronounced.

In Camus' novel, *The Fall*, a haunting laughter accompanies Jean-Baptiste Clamence across the years. He heard it first on a bridge over the Seine River where he had not tried to stop a young woman from jumping into the water and had done nothing to save her, not even reporting the incident to the police. Years later in Amsterdam, he talks on five days with a man he has met in a bar. Then he becomes ill, and his new companion comes to visit him. He tells his visitor that he has not talked at length with him for five days just for the fun of it. He has had a purpose: silencing the laughter, trying to escape the judgment he is experiencing. He has decided that the best way to escape it is to thin it out by extending the condemnation to all.[4]

Pilate, in washing his hands before that crowd, was trying to thin out the guilt for Jesus' fate. He was asking the crowd to assume the total responsibility for the execution of this innocent man. And he himself may have left that scene believing that he had shed all responsibility for what he had done.

But the fact that he did not *feel* responsible did not mean that he was *not* responsible. Feeling and actuality are not necessarily the same. One may feel responsible without really being responsible for some wrong. On the other hand, one may feel innocent enough while being as guilty as one can be.

Many things can serve to dull and deaden one's conscience, including the mere stress and strain of daily life. But it is certain, too, that this can happen when one keeps washing one's hands before one's sins. As we tell ourselves that we are not responsible, we may actually come to believe that we are not. When, like Pilate, we walk away from the wrong we have done feeling that we have no responsibility for it, we are walking toward the destination of spiritual tragedy.

But real cleansing — not exemption from responsibility, but acceptance by God in spite of our failure and sin — is available when we become honest enough to acknowledge our guilt, and when we care enough to repent of it and turn away from it. Then God comes in forgiving love, displayed so unmistakably on the Cross, to do what the water in Pilate's basin could not do. God forgives, cleansing our hearts and giving us peace within. With this cleansing comes new courage and strength, enabling us to live more responsibly before God and before the world.

The psalmist knew better than Pilate the way to cleanness; his prayer is the one we need to pray: "Have mercy on me, O God ... Wash me thoroughly from my iniquity, and cleanse me from my sin ... Create in me a clean heart, O God, and put a new and right spirit within me" (Psalm 51:1-2, 10).

---

1. C. S. Lewis, *The Screwtape Letters* (New York: The Macmillan Company, 1958), pp. 146-150.

2. Plato, *The Apology*, Great Books of the Western World edition (London, Chicago, Toronto, Geneva: Encyclopaedia Britannica, Inc., 1952), Vol. 7, p. 210.

3. Igal Mossinsohn, *Judas*, translated by Jules Harlow (New York: St. Martin's Press, 1963), p. 10.

4. Albert Camus, *The Fall* (New York: Alfred A. Knopf, 1956), p. 131.

10.

The Misdirected Tears

Luke 23:26-31

"But Jesus turned to them and said, 'Daughters of Jerusalem, do not weep for me, but weep for yourselves and for your children.'"
— Luke 23:28

Playwright Arthur Miller has a character in one of his plays say, "There are no unimportant tears."[1]

Tears were shed during Jesus' passion and death. Simon Peter, for instance, after denying that he even knew Jesus, "went out and wept bitterly" (Luke 22:62). Some might have been too shocked for tears, and might have felt as young Walter Russell Bowie did in 1894, at the age of twelve, after the funeral of his father. He and his mother were returning to their home in the old horse-drawn hack that was used at funerals, and it seemed to him "that the hoof-beats of the carriage horses were echoing in an empty world."[2] A feeling like that can dry up one's tears.

But there were some women in the crowd following the procession to Golgotha whose tears were not dried up. "They were beating their breasts and wailing for him." Peter was too far away for Jesus either to console or rebuke him, but these women were not. Stumbling along, perhaps with his eyes focused downward, when he heard their cries, he lifted his eyes and turned them toward them and spoke tenderly to them: "Daughters of Jerusalem, do not weep for me, but weep for yourselves and for your children." They were crying for the wrong person; their tears were misdirected tears.

67

The Solace They Brought

Yet Jesus must have found some consolation in them. It must have warmed his heart to know that here were a few who saw the injustice and tragedy of what was happening and felt keen sorrow because of it.

In one of Charles Schulz's *Peanuts* cartoon strips, Snoopy the beagle is sitting on top of his doghouse sniffing. He says, "What do you do? What do you do when the girl beagle you love more than anything is taken from you, and you know you'll never see her again as long as you live? What do you do?" Then in the last frame, Snoopy is pictured on the ground at his food dish eating. He says, "Back to eating!"

Was that the course these women would soon take? Would they return to their daily lives as if nothing had happened? It wasn't long before Simon Peter said to several of the other disciples, "I am going fishing," and they said, "We will go with you" (John 21:1-3). What do you do when the bottom has fallen out of life? How long do you sympathize with another's suffering? When do you dry up your tears and go on with your life? Must the tears last forever?

Harriet Beecher Stowe has a character in *Uncle Tom's Cabin* say about concern another is expressing, "I really think you can make something of that concern. Any mind that is capable of a real sorrow is capable of good."[3]

There were plenty of jeers accompanying Jesus on the way to the Cross. There was not much capacity for good in them. But these tears were different. They might or might not be dried up soon, but it must have brought some solace to Jesus to know that a few saw the tragedy of what was happening and cared enough to be pained by it. They were "capable of good" if they could feel such sorrow as that. Their tears, therefore, were not "unimportant tears." Jesus saw and appreciated them.

The Point They Missed

Still, however, he considered them to be misdirected. They missed the point of what was happening. In their eyes, Jesus had simply been overtaken by misfortune; tragedy had befallen him.

But that was not the total story. The only purpose they saw in this was the one that controlled sinful people. Jesus knew a more powerful and redemptive purpose than that was working here.

Some were saying that the law of the harvest was at work. They believed, as Goethe wrote many centuries later, that "Life's field will yield as we make it / A harvest of thorns or of flowers." Jesus had sown a certain kind of seed; now he was reaping what he had sown.

But these women could not believe that Jesus deserved what was happening to him now. They saw him stumble and fall under the weight of his cross. They saw the pallor of weakness on his cheek and the sweat of exhaustion on his brow. They remembered some things, too. They remembered his deeds of mercy. They remembered his compassion for the sick. They remembered his kind attention to their children. And they could not see justice here and could not believe Jesus was reaping the consequences of his past actions.

This meant that they were not able to make sense out of it all. They were pained by it, but they were not enlightened by it. They were saddened by it, but they were not strengthened by it. So they shed their tears.

Did they know that Jesus could have avoided or escaped what was happening, but refused to do it? Here, as always, he was acting purposefully. He was not being mastered by events; he was molding events.

Henry David Thoreau said once that if he knew for a certainty that a man was coming to his house with the conscious design of doing him good, he would run for his life![4] Thoreau was thinking, of course, of the kind of person who is determined to do the good he wants to do regardless of what the person affected thinks about it. Jesus did not operate like that. He had respect for the privacy of the human soul and for the freedom of the human will. Yet not long after these misdirected tears were shed, Simon Peter spoke of Christ as One who "went about doing good" (Acts 10:38). The whole New Testament throbs with the conviction that Christ was on a special mission on earth. He came to do good, the supreme and ultimate good: He came to save people. Somewhere along the

69

way, he began to see that this mission might take him to a cross, but if so it would not be for him just a crucifixion; it would be the crowning act of his life.

These weeping women did not have that view of the pitiful scene their eyes were beholding. They saw only the injustice and tragedy of it. Jesus knew the Divine purpose that was working through it, and so recognized their tears as misdirected tears.

The Conditions They Did Not See

It is interesting, too, that Jesus considered tears for himself less appropriate than they would have been for the women who were shedding them and for their children. That must have seemed strange to those who heard him voice that feeling. He was a convicted criminal on his way to the place of execution. They were free persons and were facing no such fate as that. Their circumstances might not have been ideal, but they were better than his. If anyone was deserving of tears of sympathy and pity, it was he, not they.

But he saw things they did not see. He, too, believed in the law of the harvest, and he knew that a people who could take the course now being taken by those sending him to a cross could expect a bitter harvest. It could not be too far away, and its terror would be so great that all tears would be needed then. This harvest came a little over a generation later when Jerusalem itself was destroyed. That was a time for tears!

Jesus also saw factors in his own situation that made it less pitiable than it might otherwise have been. One of those factors, mentioned already, was the purpose of God that was working through this event. Another was what he still had left as he was moving toward the Cross.

For one thing, he was carrying his integrity. That had not been taken from him nor discarded by him.

In Jean Anouilh's play, *Becket*, a young woman who is being treated as a thing tells Becket that he, too, belongs to a conquered race. She adds then, "But through tasting too much of the honey of life you've forgotten that even those who have been robbed of everything have one thing left to call their own."

Becket replies, "Yes, I daresay I had forgotten. There is a gap in me where honor ought to be."[5]

Jesus was about to be crucified, but there was no "gap" in him "where honor ought to be." He had not sold out. He still had his integrity. His conscience was clean and clear. He had nothing to hide and nothing of which to be ashamed, which was more than could be said of so many others. That was why those women's tears were misdirected tears.

He was carrying his faith with him to the Cross, too. He still believed in God; he believed strongly enough to continue to trust himself to God.

William Gladstone was a supporter of Dwight L. Moody's evangelistic missions in England in the late nineteenth century. Once a young Scotsman heard Gladstone exclaim: "I thank God I have lived to see the day when he should bless his church on earth by the gift of a man able to preach the gospel of Christ as we have just heard it preached!" Matthew Arnold was standing beside Gladstone, and he said, "Mr. Gladstone, I would give all I have if only I could believe it."[6]

What a faith Jesus took to the Cross! What was happening to him would have knocked the faith out of some people, but he still had his faith. So others needed those tears more than he did.

The focus of his life, the commitment of his being, had not been changed by all that had happened to him either.

More than a few have found that focus and commitment dislodged by less drastic occurrences than these. In some instances, it is the knocks of life that do the dislodging, and they decide the price is too high. Or it may be the enticements of other things that weaken their commitment to God's service; other interests become more appealing. Or perhaps they just grow negligent and fail to keep their commitment up-to-date. Something else comes in, nevertheless, and God is pushed out of the center of their lives. Then they are suitable subjects for tears, for they have weakened or abandoned the one commitment that is capable of helping them to find the meaning inherent in life, to experience the development God wants them to make, and to realize the usefulness God intends for them. Jesus still had this commitment, and so those women were crying for the wrong person.

Jesus found solace in their caring, and he did not consider their tears "unimportant tears." But he wanted them to know that Divine purpose, not blind fate, was working in this tragic event. And he wanted them to see, too, that many others, including themselves, needed their pity more than he did. For though his circumstances were deplorable indeed, he still had his integrity, he still trusted in God, and he was still totally committed to God.

Any person who still has these, regardless of his or her circumstances, is less needful of tears in his or her behalf than so many others from whose lives these are missing.

---

1. Arthur Miller, *After the Fall* (New York: Bantam Books, 1965), p. 93.

2. Walter Russell Bowie, *Learning to Live* (Nashville: Abingdon Press, 1969), p. 23.

3. Harriet Beecher Stowe, *Uncle Tom's Cabin* (New York: Harper & Row, Publishers, Perennial Classic, 1958, 1965), p. 309.

4. Henry David Thoreau, *Walden* (New York: Harper & Row, Publishers, Perennial Classic, 1958, 1965), p. 54.

5. Jean Anouilh, *Becket* (New York: Signet Books, 1960), p. 44.

6. J. C. Pollock, *Moody* (New York: The MacMillan Company, 1963), p. 154.

11.

The Rejected Drug

Matthew 27:32-37; Mark 15:21-24; Luke 23:32-38

"And they offered him wine mixed with myrrh; but he did not take it." — Mark 15:23

"They offered him wine mixed with myrrh." It was a drug, provided by kind women, maybe the same ones who wept as they followed him to Golgotha. This must have seemed to them a thoughtful and merciful thing to do. One of their proverbs said, "Give strong drink to one who is perishing, and wine to those in bitter distress; let them drink and forget their poverty, and remember their misery no more" (Proverbs 31:6-7). This would ease Jesus' pain at least a little and make his torture more bearable. Gratitude surely welled up in Jesus' heart because of this. "But he did not take it." In the Garden of Gethsemane he prayed for deliverance from another cup, if it could be God's will. It was not God's will, and so now he was about to drink that cup. But he rejected this one.

Drugs are taken for various reasons: "for the kick of it," to insure one's being "one of the crowd," to "get high," to "take a trip," to try to escape from some situation or circumstance, to ease pain. The primary purpose of those who offered the drug to Jesus was to ease his pain. No doubt similar drugs were offered to the two men crucified with him, and they may have accepted them. But Jesus did not, and we know that offered drug now as "the rejected drug."

Why did he reject it? He didn't give his reasons, so our conclusions must be based on other things we know about him, on the

Christian gospel, and on life itself. But the answer to this question may have special pertinence in a time when "the drug culture" is one of our society's most serious problems.

In The Interest Of Authentic Feeling

One of Jesus' reasons for refusing the drug must have been that he wanted to continue to feel authentically.

Sometimes persons take drugs because they want to quit feeling. They may be experiencing severe pain — physical, mental, or emotional — and they want to have that pain eased. It would be a cruel person who would say that this is never in order. One of the mercies of civilization is the medical knowledge and skill that make possible, in many instances, the relief of pain. Under ordinary circumstances no one would want to deny such relief.

Yet feeling is essential to experience. One has not really experienced something if one has not felt it. It may have happened, but one has not experienced it. There was such significance to what was happening to Jesus — indeed, to what Jesus was doing — that he did not want it to happen without his knowing about it. He wanted to feel it.

Yet this was not a psychopathic desire. He had no interest in punishing himself to satisfy some morbid need of his. He wanted to feel because his dying was not purposeless. As the writer of the Letter to the Hebrews says, he was tasting death for everyone (2:9), and it was important that he feel what was happening.

Some people take drugs, including alcohol, because they want to induce feeling, or intensify feeling, or produce a certain kind of feeling. They like what the drug does to them, at least until it wears off. But that is one of the problems with induced feeling: it doesn't last. Sooner or later one has to return to reality. Jesus simply chose not to leave reality. Throughout his life he was in tune with reality, and he had no desire for feelings that lacked reality. He wanted what he felt to be authentic.

This says something, not only about the use of drugs, but also about the kind of feeling that may be properly aimed at in worship or in other "religious" activities. It must be feeling that is authentic, not artificial. It must be in tune with reality, not removed from it.

Jesus always faced up to the truth and to the real facts in every situation. He kept doing that to the bitter end. He wanted to feel and to feel authentically. So he rejected the drug that would have deadened his feelings.

For The Sake Of Genuine Caring

Jesus may have rejected that drug also because he wanted to go on caring genuinely. The Cross itself cannot be explained apart from Christ's care for persons. He would never have gone to the Cross if he had not cared so deeply, and now on the Cross he would not seek relief from the pain which that caring cost him. That is the ultimate in caring!

In a *Calvin and Hobbes* cartoon episode, little Calvin says to his tiger friend, "I've decided to stop caring about things." He says, "If you care, you just get disappointed all the time. If you don't care, nothing matters, so you're never upset." His friend listens attentively as he continues, "From now on, my rallying cry is, 'So what?'" His friend says, "That's a tough cry to rally around." Calvin replies, "So what?"[1]

"So what?" was never Jesus' rallying cry during his years of ministry, and it would not become such as he hung on a cruel cross. Some who were there knew he cared about them, and others were to see and hear expressions of his love and concern as he hung on the cross. He prayed for his enemies, "Father, forgive them; for they do not know what they are doing" (Luke 23:34). He saw his mother standing there and asked his disciple John to take care of her (John 19:26). And to a repentant criminal dying with him, he said, "Today you will be with me in Paradise" (Luke 23:43). He whose care for people brought him to a Cross went on caring for them while he hung there.

In his poem, "The Bridge," Henry Wadsworth Longfellow tells of standing on a bridge at midnight, with a flood of thoughts sweeping over him. He recalls other times when he has stood there and wished "that the ebbing tide" would carry him away "o'er the ocean wild and wide." At such times his "heart was hot and restless" and "the burden laid upon [him] seemed greater than [he] could bear." "But now," he says,

"But now it has fallen from me,
It is buried in the sea;
And only the sorrow of others
Throws its shadow over me."[2]

That was the burden that occupied the mind and heart of Jesus on the Cross. He was not there for himself; he was not there even because he could not save himself. He was there in deep caring, in holy love, with all of his senses about him. Nothing was to keep him from continuing to care for those he came to save. Thus, as we behold him there, we see One wracked with pain but with a clear mind calling us, too, to clear-minded, warm-hearted caring for others.

He rejected the drug for the sake of genuine caring.

For The Sake Of Conscious Responsibility

He rejected it also because he wanted to continue to be consciously responsible.

Archbishop Thomas Becket, in Jean Anouilh's play, *Becket*, became an archbishop all unexpectedly. He had been carefree all of his life. He had been advisor and friend to the king, but he had not taken life very seriously. Then the king made him archbishop, and an immense sense of responsibility came upon him. Later he is talking to the king, and he says, "I felt for the first time that I was being entrusted with something, that's all — there in that empty cathedral, somewhere in France, that day when you ordered me to take up this burden. I was a man without honor. And suddenly I found it — one I never imagined would ever become mine — the honor of God." And he began to live as a man under responsibility.[3]

Early in his presidency, John F. Kennedy was asked what presidential label he expected to wear. He replied, "I hope to be responsible."[4]

That was what Jesus was doing on the Cross. Indeed, it was what he had been doing all of his life, even as early as the age of twelve when he said to his bewildered and worried parents after they had searched and found him in the Temple in Jerusalem, "Did you not know that I must be about my Father's business?" (Luke

2:49 NKJV). He was supremely about that business now, and he would do it in full consciousness until he could say, "It is finished" (John 19:30). So he rejected the drug that would have dulled his consciousness.

Frequently some wrong is done, some sin committed, some injury inflicted, because a person is "not himself or herself." The person may be under the influence of alcohol or some other drug, and so does things he or she would never do without that influence.

A young man with a broken heart came to his minister one day and asked him to read a letter from the girl he loved. The letter told of a night of debauchery that had resulted from alcohol being poured into her beverage without her knowledge. Her conduct after that was totally irresponsible. Another young man, in the depths of misery, told of a sin he had committed, and said, "I would not have done it if I had not been drinking."

If one commits a crime while one's mind is drugged, the defense counsel may plead diminished responsibility. But one's responsibility under God does not begin at the point of conduct harmful to others or to oneself. It begins a great deal earlier than that!

Jesus, of course, was not in danger of doing evil when he refused that drug; he was in the act of doing the supreme good, and he wanted to do it deliberately and consciously. So he rejected the offered drug.

In 1931, long before the modern proliferation of the use of illegal drugs, Aldous Huxley, in *Brave New World*, envisioned a society where people were so conditioned that they could not help doing what they ought to do. The drug, soma, made this possible. There was always soma to calm one's anger, to reconcile one to one's enemies, to make one patient and long-suffering. Huxley has the Controller of this "brave new world" say, "Anybody can be virtuous now."[5]

But is that really virtue? Is goodness one does not choose really goodness? Jesus chose the good he did on Golgotha.

"There isn't any need for a civilized [person] to bear anything that's seriously unpleasant."[6] That is the philosophy of Huxley's drug-saturated "brave new world." But Christ operated on a different philosophy. He rejected the idea that nothing good could come

77

out of pain. He knew there could be redemptive power in it. Indeed, the author of the Letter to the Hebrews said that "he learned obedience through what he suffered" (Hebrews 5:8). So he chose to bear the pain of Calvary with all of his senses about him. He wanted to feel and to feel authentically.

He had lived a caring life. It was caring that had brought him to the Cross, and he wanted to go on caring to the end. So he refused the drug that might have eased his pain a little but might also have moved him to say, "So what?"

Christ lived always as a man under responsibility — responsibility to God and for his fellow human beings. The offered drug might have deadened his sense of responsibility, and since he wanted to be responsible even as he died, he would not take the drug.

Across the centuries then that rejected drug sends its message to us. It tells us of the redemption there can be in pain. It calls us to guard against deadening influences — of whatever kind or nature — that would keep us from feeling the pains of others and caring genuinely about them. And it calls us to avoid anything that would keep us from authentically bearing the label, "Responsible."

1. *Calvin and Hobbes*, in *The Atlanta Journal and Constitution*, January 2, 1993.

2. *The Complete Poems of Henry Wadsworth Longfellow* (Cutchogue, New York: Buccaneer Books, 1993), pp. 63-64.

3. Jean Anouilh, *Becket* (New York: Signet, 1960), p. 114.

4. William Manchester, *Portrait of a President* (New York: McFadden Books, 1964, copyright 1962 by William Manchester), p. 130.

5. Aldous Huxley, *Brave New World* (New York: Bantam Books, 1953), pp. 161-162.

6. *Ibid.*

12.

The Torn Curtain

Matthew 27:45-54; Mark 15:33-39; Luke 23:44-49

"At that moment the curtain of the temple was torn in two, from top to bottom."   — Matthew 27:51

Plagued on every side by loss, suffering, and sorrow, righteous Job cried out: "Oh, that I knew where I might find him, that I might come even to his dwelling!" (Job 23:3). He wanted to know where he could find God. The Hebrew people believed they had the answer to Job's question. They said that God's dwelling was in Jerusalem, in a special room in the Temple there.

This room was only a small part of the Temple complex, but it was the most important part. There were steps leading up to it from the place where sacrifices were made on a daily basis. That place itself was a Holy Place, but this room was the Most Holy Place or Holy of Holies. Yet so far as human activity was concerned, it was a seldom-used room.

The only person who could enter the Holy of Holies was the High Priest, the spiritual leader of the Jewish people, and he could enter it on only one day of the year, the Day of Atonement (now called Yom Kippur). Actually, he entered the Holy of Holies three times on the Day of Atonement. On his first entrance, he used a censer to cense the shrine to protect himself from the Divine mystery. On his second entrance he carried a vessel of blood from a slain bull and sprinkled the blood on specified places. On his third entrance he carried the blood from a slain goat, sprinkling it, too, at designated points.

79

Originally the ark of the covenant, which had meant so much to the Hebrews in their early history as a people, had been placed in this room. But the ark had been lost when the Babylonians destroyed the Temple in 587 B.C. The significance attached to the ark explains why the Holy of Holies was so important. The ark was a small portable box, with handles for carrying and with a cover made of gold and called "the mercy seat." This ark represented the presence of God, and the room in which it was placed was thought of as the special dwelling place of God.

But God was not to be approached in this Most Holy Place by ordinary people. The High Priest, the one person who could approach God there, did so as the representative of the people, and he came with sacrifices for them, seeking Divine forgiveness for them and the smile of God upon their lives. He and his people could be assured of this if the rites were carried out properly.

It was always a momentous occasion when the Day of Atonement came and the High Priest, in his splendid robes, ascended to the Holy of Holies. But something separated him from the inside of that room. It was a fine linen curtain of blue, purple, and scarlet colors, hanging over the entrance to the room, shutting the light out of it and obscuring everyone's view of the inside of it. It was there as a warning against intrusion upon the privacy of God and as a symbol of the division that existed between God and people.

Three of the Gospels — Matthew, Mark, and Luke — mention this curtain in connection with the crucifixion of Jesus. They say there was darkness over the land, and that as Jesus breathed his last breath, "the curtain of the Temple was torn in two, from the top to the bottom." Whether we are to understand this as an actual historical occurrence or as a theological statement, we must not miss the good news in it — the good news of a torn curtain!

An Unconfined God

It speaks to us, for one thing, of an unconfined God.

A magnificent prayer offered by Solomon at the dedication of the first Temple acknowledges that God is too great to be contained in a building. "But will God indeed dwell on the earth?" Solomon asks. Then his prayer continues, "Even heaven and the highest heaven cannot contain you, much less this house that I have built!" Yet it was believed, even centuries later, that God had promised, "My name shall be there" (1 Kings 8:27-30). At the very time of Jesus' crucifixion, there were several million people who would have answered the question "Where can we find God?" by saying, "In Jerusalem, in the Temple in Jerusalem."

But where would you say that God was on that day? There was quietness in that innermost room of the Temple. Surely that was a good place for God to be — removed from the noise and dirtiness and turmoil of the world. But the early Christians came to believe that God had been present at another place, too. It was a place of ugliness and pain and death. Yet a hardened soldier, as he stood there watching three men die and listening especially to the gasping words of one of the men, said: "Truly this man was God's Son!" (Matthew 27:54; Mark 15:39).

Matthew Brady, the noted lawyer in the play *Inherit the Wind*, is a pathetic figure as the play comes to an end. Drummond, the defense counsel, has won over him but cannot rejoice in his victory. He says, "A giant once lived in that body. But Matt Brady got lost. Because he was looking for God too high up and too far away."[1]

Where should one look for God? God is often experienced in some place set aside as a sanctuary. But God is never confined to the places where people think God ought to be. God may be in the ugly, the unpleasant, the painful, the distasteful, as well as in the beautiful, the pleasurable, the joyful.

Harvard psychiatrist Robert Coles tells about working with Dorothy Day's Catholic Worker soup kitchen as a young man. One afternoon, after he and several others had struggled for some time with a "wino," a "Bowery bum," an angry, cursing, hostile man with virtually no teeth and bloodshot eyes, Dorothy Day said to them: "For all we know he might be God himself come here to test us, so let us treat him as an honored guest and look at his face as if it is the most beautiful one we can imagine."[2]

Dr. Coles said he had difficulty thinking of that man's face as the face of God. Well, where would God's face be? God is an unconfined God, and sometimes abides in unlikely persons and unexpected places. God is too great to be kept within one place or one type of place. Neither can God be confined to a creed or doctrinal statement or a particular set of circumstances. The torn curtain tells us of an unconfined God.

An Illumined God

The torn curtain also symbolizes for us illumination of the mystery of God.

There were no windows or skylights in the Holy of Holies, and the curtain over the entrance shut out much of the light that would have come in through that opening. But then when the curtain was torn from the top to the bottom and the sun appeared again, light began to illuminate that dark room.

Mystery was associated with the Holy of Holies. That was one of the reasons why enemies who gained possession of the Temple always wanted to venture into it. They had heard about it, and they wanted to see if God really dwelt there, or they wanted to demonstrate that God did not dwell there.

The Second Book of Maccabees records an interesting story, most likely a legend, about a foreign invader, a man by the name of Heliodorus, who got the beating of his life from a strange horse and three armored men when he tried to invade the Temple. When his king, Antiochus Epiphanes of Syria, asked him what sort of man would be suitable to send to Jerusalem another time, he answered: "If you have any enemy or plotter against your government, send him there, for you will get him back thoroughly flogged, if he survives at all; for there is certainly some power of God about the place" (2 Maccabees 3). There were many questions about the nature of this "power." God's being, like the Holy of Holies itself, was surrounded by mystery. Indeed, that must always be the case, for God is too great to be comprehended fully by finite human minds. In one of his sermons, Saint Augustine said to his congregation: "Since it is God we are speaking of, you do not understand it. If you could understand it, it would not be God."[3]

But there is such a thing as mystery being illuminated, and that is what happened at the Cross. The torn curtain symbolizes an illumined mystery. The mystery is still there, but light has been thrown on it. Nothing else in all the universe nor in human history so illumines the being of God as does that Cross. No wonder John Bowring could sing: "From the cross the radiance streaming / Adds more luster to the day."[4]

It makes a difference, it "adds more luster to the day," to see the heart of God as revealed by Christ on the Cross. "No one has greater love than this, to lay down one's life for one's friends" (John 15:13).

An Accessible God

The torn curtain speaks of an accessible God, one who can be approached by any person in the world.

Jesus himself never entered the Holy of Holies. If he had tried to do so, he would have been put to death. That was too holy a place for an ordinary person to enter.

It was both the condition of humanity and the nature of God that forbade this. Humankind was sinful, and the holiness of God made sin repugnant in God's eyes. God's distaste for sin was so great that something had to be done to make persons acceptable to God. That was the function of the sacrifices, especially the blood sacrifices carried into the Holy of Holies by the High Priest on the Day of Atonement.

But Jesus' death eliminated the necessity of animal sacrifices. Centuries before, a psalmist had said, "The sacrifice acceptable to God is a broken spirit; a broken and contrite heart, O God, you will not despise" (Psalm 51:17). The judge and prophet Samuel had asked, "Has the Lord as great delight in burnt offerings and sacrifices, as in obeying the voice of the Lord?" Then he had said, "Surely, to obey is better than sacrifice, and to heed than the fat of rams" (1 Samuel 15:22). Yet sacrifice had continued to be of utmost importance. In Hebrew understanding, something had to be done to hide the sins of persons from the eyes of God, making it possible for them to be at one with God. So for centuries, relationship with God had been regulated and determined by ritual and had been mediated by a special class of people, the priests.

Jesus' death on the Cross showed God in a new light. God was not waiting in some distant heaven, or in some special place on earth, for people to offer the proper sacrifice or to have one offered for them that would make them presentable to God. God was coming to meet persons, as a father meeting a returning prodigal son, bearing in the Divine heart a pain and anguish that required for its relief only a broken spirit, contriteness of heart, sincere sorrow for one's sin.

The writer of the Letter to the Hebrews pictures Jesus entering the Holy of Holies while on his Cross. He had not entered it before, but, symbolically, now he did. The High Priest had entered it every year, but once was enough for Jesus. "He entered once for all into the Holy Place, not with the blood of goats and calves, but with his own blood, thus obtaining eternal redemption" (Hebrews 9:12).

We still are not to think lightly of our sins or of the holiness of God. But we can approach God with confidence, with assurance of forgiveness and acceptance, because of the Cross of Christ. As the author of Hebrews put it, "Since we have confidence to enter the sanctuary by the blood of Jesus, by the new and living way that he opened for us through the curtain ... let us approach with a true heart in full assurance of faith ..." (Hebrews 10:19-22).

That Temple curtain was no longer appropriate after Jesus died on the Cross. It symbolized a separated God, an unapproachable God. But the Cross speaks of a seeking God, a suffering God, an accessible God.

A curtain torn by a cross! That torn curtain tells us of a God too great to be confined in creeds, places, rituals, or circumstances. The light that moves through that torn curtain comes from the Cross, illuminating the mystery of God and showing us what we most need to know about the being of God. And it speaks of accessibility, assuring us of an open way to the Divine presence.

Thank God for the torn Temple curtain!

---

1. Jerome Lawrence and Robert E. Lee, *Inherit the Wind* (New York, London, Toronto: Random House, Inc., 1955, Bantam Pathfinder edition, 1963), p. 114.

2. Robert Coles, *The Spiritual Life of Children* (Boston: Houghton Mifflin Company, 1990), pp. 67-68.

3. Garry Wills, *Saint Augustine* (New York: Penguin Putnam, Inc., copyright 1999 by Garry Wills), p. xii.

4. John Bowring, "In the Cross of Christ I Glory," in *The United Methodist Hymnal* (Nashville: The United Methodist Publishing House, 1989), Number 195.

13.

The Unused Spices

Matthew 28:1-10; Mark 16:1-8; Luke 23:55—24:10

"When the Sabbath was over, Mary Magdalene, and Mary the mother of James, and Salome bought spices, so that they might go and anoint him."
— Mark 16:1

Spices were important commodities in the ancient world. Fragrant vegetable products, they were used for cosmetics, as sacred oil and incense for worship, as perfume, and for burial purposes. Extensive trade in spices was carried on, and one who had large quantities of spices was considered wealthy.

Jews, like other peoples in their region, used spices in preparing bodies for burial. The purpose was for ceremonial purification rather than for preservation of the bodies.

It is not spices in general though that I have in mind now; it is particular spices. These had been purchased by some women, friends of Jesus, and were brought by them on Easter morning to the tomb where Jesus' body had been laid. They intended to anoint his body, but when they reached the tomb, his body was not there.

What happened to those spices then? Did the women, in their surprise and fright, simply drop them outside the tomb and forget about them? The spices were expensive; did they return them to the shop where they had purchased them and get their money back? Did they use them for some other purpose? We don't know; it really doesn't matter. What does matter is that they were no longer needed for the purpose for which they were originally intended. They were new spices then, and were to have been used immediately. But they were still unused after the eastern sun had risen high in the sky.

Symbol Of Love

Those unused spices are a symbol of love. They were bought by Mary Magdalene, Mary the mother of James, and Salome. We know little about these women, except that they were among those who followed Jesus and helped to finance his ministry (Matthew 27:55-56; Mark 15:40-41; Luke 8:1-3). Mark's Gospel tells us that Jesus had cast seven demons out of Mary Magdalene (Mark 16:9). This led Andrew Lloyd Webber and Tim Rice to have her sing in *Jesus Christ — Superstar* about how she has been changed, "really changed," so that when she sees herself she seems like someone else. And she exclaims, "I love him so."[1]

Perhaps the others had similar reasons for loving him. At any rate, it is not likely they would have come to his tomb on that first day of the week to anoint his body with spices if they had not loved him. Those spices are a symbol of the love they had for him.

Jesus had known so much of hate in those last days of his life, but through it all he must have been sure of the love of these devoted women. At least a little joy must have welled up in his heart at the thought of their love for him.

Before Augustine became a Christian, he had a dear friend whom he lost in death, and it seemed for a while that he himself could not continue to live. He was so close to his friend that he felt that their souls were "one soul in two bodies." He later wrote in his *Confessions*, "Therefore was my life a horror to me, because I would not live halved."[2]

Those women must have felt something like that, too. In Christ they had found a love that had transformed their lives, and they had come to love him in return. He meant so much to them that it must have seemed that they were now "halved." It was loving hearts that carried them to his tomb that morning. Their unused spices are a symbol of their love.

Evidence Of Faithfulness

Those spices are also evidence of faithfulness. When Jesus was alive, these women had attended faithfully to his needs. Part of the time they had traveled with him, and from their own possessions they had contributed to his necessities and to those of his disciples. Their faces were among those seen at the Crucifixion. They had done all they could do, and now they watched from a distance, with bleeding hearts, as he suffered and died. They came closer when he was taken down from the Cross, and they followed to the garden where he was entombed. The Sabbath was at hand then, and they could do nothing else for him until it was past. But then they came again, in faithfulness, to anoint his body with spices they had bought. Those spices are evidence of their faithfulness to Jesus.

Not everyone values faithfulness that much. We want to be happy; we want our rights; we want to advance in the world; we want to be liked, to be popular; we want to be healthy and prosperous. But what about being faithful — faithful to our duties, faithful to our vows and commitments, faithful to our country, to our church, to our God? Just where does faithfulness fit into our scale of priorities?

When Adlai Stevenson was running for President of the United States in 1952, he spoke at the dedication of a monument to Elijah Lovejoy in Alton, Illinois. Lovejoy was a Presbyterian minister and anti-slavery editor who was shot to death on November 7, 1837, while trying to protect his printing press from a mob. Mr. Stevenson quoted the words Elijah Lovejoy spoke to the mob just before he was shot: "I am impelled in the course I have taken because I fear God. As I shall answer to God in the great day, I dare not abandon my sentiments nor cease in all proper ways to propagate them. I can die at my post; but I cannot desert it."[3]

Few, if any, of us are fated to die as a result of faithfulness. But our lives would make more of a difference in the world if we were that faithful.

Samuel Johnson, the eighteenth century English conversationalist and literary figure, wrote a great many prayers. The manuscript of one of his birthday prayers, written on September 18,

89

1758, has these words below the prayer: "This year I hope to learn diligence."[4]

Diligence is worth learning, but what about learning faithfulness, too? We could do with a good supply of that. The spices those women brought to Jesus' tomb were evidence of their faithfulness. Somewhere along the way, they had learned faithfulness. May God help us to learn it, too.

Token Of Triumph

Consider, too, that those unused spices are a token of triumph. If it had been necessary for the women to use them that morning, there would be nothing to say about Christ's triumph. But they didn't have to use them. Christ had been raised, triumphant over sin, over evil, and over death. Those spices then, unused, are a token of his triumph.

There is a story from India about the Buddha being stopped one day by a young woman who had long been childless and who, after many years, had given birth to a son. The child, playing among the bushes, was bitten by a poisonous snake and died. Pleading with the Buddha to restore her son to life, she received the answer: "Go, and bring me some mustard seeds from the home of people who are not mourning a death." Life expectancy was much lower then than it is now, and the infant mortality rate was tragically high. The mother began to wander about, in search of such a home, but after many years returned empty-handed. Seeing her return, the Buddha said: "When you departed you thought that you and you alone were the only one who had ever suffered a loss through death. Now that you have returned, you know differently. Now you know that the law of death governs us all."[5]

That is why we need an authoritative word about it, and Christ's resurrection gives us that word. No wonder Principal James Denney said, "The Gospel cannot be described at all unless it is described as a victory over death as well as sin."[6]

Financier Bernard Baruch tells about his father calling him and his brothers into his study once and asking them to promise that when he lay dying they would not allow their mother to send for a rabbi to say any final Jewish prayer. They promised, and when he was 81 and had a stroke and was dying, they had to say, "No," when their mother tried to get them to call the rabbi. Just a few days before he had reminded them of their earlier promise, adding, "The last thing I can do for you boys is to show you how to die."[7]

Jesus showed us that twenty centuries ago. But he did more: He robbed death of its power and took away its final threat. He triumphed over it, and he promises us victory over it, too. That is why we may hope to "find, when ended is the page, / Death but a tavern on our pilgrimage."[8]

Those unused spices are a token of triumph!

Stimulant To Hope

Therefore, they may also be a stimulant to hope. Imagine the hopes that must have come alive in the hearts of those women when they found that they did not need those spices! They had thought that Jesus' companionship was lost to them forever, but now that dead hope became a living hope. With Jesus' crucifixion, they had despaired of the Kingdom of God becoming a reality on any time schedule that would make any difference to them. But now they could pray again with hope for the coming of the Kingdom.

As they had shared in Jesus' ministry, they had felt the thrill of being involved in something that put meaning and purpose and joy into life. The Cross ended all that, but when they did not need to use those spices, they could dare to hope again that life would once more possess the wonder and excitement and meaning they had so recently come to find in it. There was a lot they did not understand as they turned away from that tomb, but hope was beginning to come alive in their hearts once more.

Hope is such an essential ingredient for meaningful living. When hope is taken out of life, the lift is taken out of it, too, and life becomes a burden to be borne. But when hope is alive and flourishing, there is something to draw one forward and to give buoyancy to existence.

But hope has numerous foes. Circumstances can dislodge it. Broken or strained relationships can overpower it. Disappointments, griefs, failures can smother it. But the resurrection of Jesus proclaims the presence and power of God in the midst of life's troubles, turmoils, and tragedies. God can bring good out of evil, victory out of defeat, life out of death, hope out of despair. That is why those unused spices may be stimulants to hope!

If those particular spices had been intended for one of the other common uses of spices, they would have no significance for us today. But they were not, and so they symbolize a love that stayed alive in the midst of death, and they call us to bring to Christ the affection of our souls, the devotion of our hearts, the consecration of our wills. They give evidence of a faithfulness that does not quit, reminding us of the need for the developing and strengthening of faithfulness in us — faithfulness to Christ, to persons, to vital causes, to ideals and convictions. Those unused spices are tokens of Christ's victory over death. Because of that victory, "chords that were broken" within us may "vibrate once more," and we may know what it is to live in the hope that the Resurrection makes possible.

1. Andrew Lloyd Webber and Tim Rice, *Jesus Christ — Superstar*.

2. Augustine, *The Confessions* (Great Books edition, Vol. 18), p. 22.

3. Cited by Clarence E. Macartney, *The Woman of Tekoah* (New York and Nashville: Abingdon Press, 1955), p. 31.

4. Elton Trueblood, editor, *Doctor Johnson's Prayers* (London: SCM Press Limited, 1947), p. 24.

5. Martin Diskin and Hans Guggenheim, "The Child and Death as Seen in Different Cultures," in *Explaining Death to Children*, edited by Earl A. Grollman (Boston: Beacon Press, 1967), pp. 122-123.

6. W. Robertson Nicoll, editor, *Letters of Principal James Denney* (London, New York, Toronto: Hodder and Stoughton Limited, n.d.), p. 193.

7. Bernard Baruch, *My Own Story* (New York: Pocket Books, Inc., Cardinal Giant edition, 1958), pp. 88-89.

8. John Masefield, "The Word," in *Poems* (New York: The Macmillan Company, 1951), p. 71.

14.

The Misplaced Christ

John 20:1-18

"They have taken away my Lord, and I do not know where they have laid him." — John 20:13

The various Gospel accounts of the first Easter bear similarities to each other, but there are also interesting and significant differences in them. The Gospel of John, for instance, instead of telling about several women coming to the tomb on the first day of the week, individualizes the account and centers it around one woman, Mary Magdalene.

Mary, of all women, is one we would have expected to come to Jesus' tomb on an errand of love. She had plenty of reason to love Jesus, for he had done something for her that had radically transformed her life. We are not sure just what her condition was, but we are told that Jesus cast seven demons out of her (Luke 8:1-3; Mark 16:9). In those times, demons were associated not only with physical ailments, but also with moral and spiritual defects. So shame would most likely have been associated with her condition. Jesus gave her wholeness of body and spirit, restoring a sense of dignity and worth, and gave her a new purpose for living and new motivation and strength for such living. We are not surprised to see her coming very early in the morning to Jesus' tomb.

She is surprised, however, and disturbed as well, not to find Jesus' body in the tomb. In great distress, she hurries to find Peter and John, saying to them, "They have taken the Lord out of the tomb, and we do not know where they have laid him." In her view, upset though she is, it is a simple matter of someone having misplaced, moved to another location, the body of her crucified Lord.

Peter and John, not yet having the first kindlings of resurrection faith, share her concern and rush, even run, to the tomb to see for themselves. John is convinced by what he sees that it is not just a matter of Jesus' body having been misplaced. He believes that Jesus has been resurrected. The Gospel of John does not tell us whether or not Peter shares John's faith, but soon they return to their places of residence.

But Mary does not go with them. Instead, she tarries, leaning against the outside of the tomb, weeping warm tears of distress and occasionally looking inside the tomb in the hope that she has been mistaken.

Through her tears she sees heavenly messengers who ask her why she is weeping. She replies, "They have taken away my Lord, and I do not know where they have laid him." Then she turns around and sees someone standing nearby. She says to him, "Sir, if you have carried him away, tell me where you have laid him, and I will take him away."

The only possibility she could entertain was that the body of Jesus had been moved. In a moment a new possibility would dawn on her mind, but now she was obsessed with the thought of a misplaced Christ.

Misdirected Searching

One problem was that her searching was misdirected. She was trying to find Jesus where she thought he ought to be. He had been left in a certain place; she had seen his body placed there, and she thought he ought still to be there. She expected him to stay put, but he did not!

Is that not an expectation commonly held by us, too? We are not dealing with a dead body now, of course, but still we may expect that Christ will not move around too much. We want to keep him located where we can find him easily, which may mean in some quiet secluded garden, rather than in the thick of our common life.

But Christ won't stay put. He keeps bursting out of the bonds in which we try to bind him. He will not be confined to particular places. He will not be excluded from vital issues. He will not be restrained from selected situations. And if we assume that he will, we may find ourselves searching for what seems to be a misplaced Christ.

Mary's search was misdirected also because her focus was on the past. She is not to be faulted for that; such would be thoughtlessly cruel. It was because Christ had acted redemptively in her life in the past that she cared enough to tend his lifeless body now when there was no longer anything else he could do. She had no reason for thinking of him except in terms of what was past. But before long she knew him, not just as a lovely life of the past, but as a living presence encountering her anew.

We have the Easter story for our enlightenment, as Mary did not, but we, too, tend to look for Christ only in the past. We need to see and to know him there, but the Resurrection tells us that Christ cannot be kept there. He is our eternal contemporary. He keeps bursting out of the grave clothes of the dead past and confronting us as a living presence. To look for him, therefore, only in the past is to be misdirected in our searching.

Delayed Recognition

Dr. G. H. C. MacGregor called this story of Mary Magdalene's experience with the risen Christ "the greatest recognition scene in all literature."[1] But when Christ appeared to her, it was at first a case of mistaken identity and of delayed recognition. Mary thought he was the gardener!

Two related factors delayed her recognition of Christ. One was her unexpectancy, and the other was her preoccupation.

Mary wanted to find Jesus, but she did not expect him to be walking around outside that tomb. When she had first come to Joseph's garden, she had expected to find Jesus' body in the tomb where it had been placed. But when it was not there, she did not know what to expect. So Jesus' appearance to her was totally unexpected, and at first she did not recognize him.

Carl Sandburg has a poem about a college teacher who has earned a doctor's degree from the University of Heidelberg, and has had a variety of experiences far removed from the university setting. Once, for instance, he lived for six weeks in a tent looking in the face of the Great Sphinx of Egypt. One morning as he was shaving, he asked the Sphinx to tell him something worth telling. The Sphinx broke its long silence and said: "Don't expect too much."[2]

"If you don't expect anything, you won't be disappointed," it is said. But that is a pretty drab philosophy by which to try to live. Yet at times, in part at least because of past disappointments, we may allow a spirit of unexpectancy to settle down over our lives, and Christ may be close at hand without our recognizing him.

Mary's preoccupation also contributed to the delay in her recognition of Jesus. It is true that she was there because she wanted to find Christ, but she was so preoccupied with the misplaced Christ that for a moment she could not recognize the living Christ.

Mary was preoccupied with a problem. She was blinded by her tears, absorbed in her grief. The Christian gospel tells us that Christ is eternally near, but it is not always easy to recognize him when life bears down upon us — "when burdens press and cares distress."

There are so many things with which we may become preoccupied: our burdens and problems, our regrets, our guilt, our dreams and ambitions, pleasures, making a living, getting an education, succeeding, surviving ...

In T. S. Eliot's play, *Murder in the Cathedral*, the tragic end is approaching for Archbishop Thomas Becket. He has anticipated it, but still finds its approach to be unexpected. He says that when the "moment foreseen" comes, we are not expecting it because we are "engrossed with matters of other urgency."[3]

So often that is the way it is with Christ's coming, too. He would not have us to be perpetual idlers, yet sometimes our preoccupation — perhaps even with good things — prevents us from recognizing his living presence with us.

Unexpected Finding

But the gospel part of this matchless story of Mary's search for the misplaced Christ is that in the end it was not Mary who found Christ, but Christ who found Mary. Mary had been seeking him to no avail; then she discovered that he was seeking her, and she was found of him. His search for us always precedes our search for him, and when we find him, we discover that we have been found.

This is a marvelous gospel truth, permeating the whole of Jesus' mission and message. He talked about a seeking God, and his own life gave evidence of the depth of that conviction. John's story about the blind man whose healing by Jesus resulted in his being excommunicated from the synagogue is one illustration of this. John says that when Jesus learned that he had been cast out of the synagogue, he went looking for him and found him (John 9:35). He came to seek and to save the lost!

This is good news! If you are astray from God, you can be sure that God is not far from you. When it seems that you have lost all contact with God, when your spiritual life is dim, thin, drab, or meager, God has not gone off somewhere and left you alone. God comes seeking you in your lostness. And there is hope for the reestablishment of relationship with God, because God has already taken the initiative to find you and to restore you to Divine fellowship.

I remember seeing a cartoon once that pictured a man looking at a bulletin board that was supposed to have a "thought for the day" on it. It was a holiday, and the sign read: "Due to the holiday, there is no thought for the day." It may seem at times as if God has taken a holiday or extended vacation, but Jesus' coming to Mary outside the garden tomb tells us of a God who arises in the midst of death and seeks us out even in our sorrow and trouble and doubt and despair.

This means that at no time or in any place are we hopelessly shut off from God. Hence Pierre Teilhard de Chardin's New Year's wish for a friend is always possible of fulfillment for any of us. He wrote, "May the new year be kind to you — that is, brimful of the presence of God."[4] If our own faithfulness were all we had to depend upon, our prospects would be dim indeed. But God in Christ keeps arising in the graveyard of our doubts, failures, despairs, broken promises, and dreams, and he finds us and calls us by name and gives us hope and joy again!

"They have taken away my Lord, and I do not know where they have laid him." To Mary he was the misplaced Christ. He may be that to us, too, at times. We look for him but cannot find him. We long for his fellowship, but he is nowhere to be found. What then?

Perhaps we should consider whether or not our search is misdirected. We may have expected Christ to stay where we put him, while he keeps bursting the bonds we try to wrap around him. We may be focusing on the past, while he wants to be a living presence with us. We may not be recognizing him because of the haze of unexpectancy or the blur of preoccupation.

In such times, it might be helpful if we would go back in memory and imagination to that moment in Joseph's garden when the risen Christ found this weeping friend and called her by name, and she was "surprised by joy,"[5] the joy of the living presence of her resurrected Lord. He arises in the midst of any death that may surround us, too, and if we have ears to hear, we may hear him call our name, as he comes to us with love and forgiveness and joy and strength.

---

1. G. H. C. MacGregor, *The Gospel of John* (New York and London: Harper and Brothers Publishers, 1929), p. 358.

2. Carl Sandburg, *The People, Yes* (New York: Harcourt, Brace and Co., 1936), p. 20.

3. T. S. Eliot, "Murder in the Cathedral," in *The Complete Poems and Plays* (New York: Harcourt, Brace & World, Inc., 1962), p. 203.

4. Pierre Teilhard de Chardin, *Letters from a Traveler* (New York and London: Harper & Row, Publishers; London: William Collins Sons & Co., Ltd., 1962), p. 296.

5. Title of C. S. Lewis' autobiography (New York: Harcourt, Brace and Company, 1955).

15.

The Idle Tale

Matthew 28:1-10; Mark 16:1-11; Luke 24:1-12

"But these words seemed to them an idle tale, and they did not believe them."   — Luke 24:11

On the tiptoe of expectation is hardly the way to describe the mood of the disciples on the first Easter morning. They were not expectant; they were despondent. They were not hopeful; they were pessimistic. And so the news that Jesus had risen from the dead took them completely by surprise. They thought it was an "idle tale," or as other translations put it, "nonsense."

The proclamation of the Resurrection was to meet with that kind of response from many in the years ahead, but why from Jesus' own disciples? These were the men who had known him most intimately. They had had the best opportunity to become acquainted with his thought and message. He had even talked to them about what was going to happen. Then they didn't believe it when they were told that it had happened. It seems strange indeed!

But it has to be kept in mind that the Gospels were written after the Resurrection, not before it. This means that they were written in the light of that momentous event and that the writers saw and heard Jesus, not just as he had been seen and heard during his actual ministry, but also as he was revealed by his Resurrection.

Isn't it true that we often see persons in a different perspective after they are no longer among us? Their words and deeds take on new meaning in the light of their changed status. How much more this would have been true in regard to Jesus. The disciples knew it was no ordinary person with whom they were associating. But when they were convinced of his Resurrection, they began to see all he had said and done in the light of that event. When we read some of the things they remembered his having said to them, we wonder how dull they could have been not to be expecting him to arise. But they were just ordinary people like us, slow to see and to comprehend spiritual truth. So Jesus' Resurrection caught them by surprise, and at first they could not believe it. It seemed to them an idle tale.

Mocking Empty Hearts

As such it seemed also a mockery of their empty hearts.

Helen Keller was writing once about the tendency to see in the world around one only a mirror reflecting one's own feelings and ideas. She said that some people "look within themselves — and find nothing! Therefore they conclude that there is nothing outside themselves either."[1]

But the emptiness in the hearts of those disciples was based on reality. It was caused by actual happenings outside themselves. Something had happened in their world, and it had made a difference in their hearts. Where there had been meaning and joy, there was now emptiness and despondency.

Some of this nation's darkest days were those following the assassination of President John F. Kennedy. As his widow brooded over what had happened, she mentioned the sadness he had known and said: "But now he will never know more — not age, nor stagnation, nor despair, nor crippling illness, nor loss of any more people he loved. His high noon kept all the freshness of the morning — and he died then, never knowing disillusionment."[2]

Such was not the case with these disciples of Jesus. They had known a high noon that had kept all the freshness of the morning. Then suddenly the sun had gone down for them, leaving them in darkness, bewildered, disillusioned, empty-hearted.

To treat such a feeling lightly or to promise relief for it falsely is cruel mockery of it. They had had enough pain already. What had happened to Jesus and their own conduct through it all had about done them in. Surely no one would be heartless enough to deceive them about something like this. To tell them that the Christ

102

they had loved so dearly was alive again, if untrue, was a mockery of their empty hearts.

Mending Broken Dreams

Yet that was the beginning of the mending of their broken dreams.

What great dreams had possessed the hearts and minds of Jesus' disciples! In company with Jesus they had envisioned great things. At times some of them had become a little too personally ambitious in their dreaming, as when James and John set their eyes on the positions of greatest honor in the expected kingdom (Matthew 20:20-28). But no doubt they had dreamed of peace and justice and righteousness, too. There was no limit to what they might achieve under the leadership of their new Master.

Yet dreams are sometimes fragile things that can be broken, and that is what happened to the disciples' dreams at Golgotha. They were shattered to pieces, and they were left with the debris. What do you do with a broken dream?

Edgar A. Guest may declare that "one broken dream is not the end of dreaming," and that the stars are still gleaming "beyond the storm and tempest," and may advise that one should still build castles, though the castles fall.[3] But how do you manage to see beyond the storm and tempest to where the "stars are gleaming"? How do you keep building castles when the King is dead?

Edwin Markham, in his poem "The Dream," notes that it is easy to dream in youth, but emphasizes the importance of continuing to dream as life moves on. It is a greater thing, he says, "to fight life through / And say at the end, 'The dream is true!' "[4]

Really, youth and age were not involved in the inability of the disciples to keep their dreams alive. An event of earth-shattering significance had brought them to the point where they had to say, "The dream is not true!"

Then all unexpectedly the mending process began. It was not anyone's exhortation on the importance of dreaming that started it though. They did not just decide to "get their chins up" and think positively about life. They did not decide to live in the present, forgetful of the past. Rather, they heard some good news. If what they heard was true, there was no longer any reason to doubt that their dreams could be fulfilled.

Christ had been both the inspirer and the basis of their dreaming, and if he were alive again, they could pick up their dreams and believe in them again and say with real conviction, "The dream is true!"

That idle tale started the mending of their broken dreams.

Renewing Weakened Purposes

This means that their weakened purposes began to be renewed also.

Novelist Graham Greene tells of his feelings, as a young man, at his first confession preceding his baptism. He found the confession, which was supposed to cover the whole of his previous life, to be a humiliating ordeal. He says he had not yet become hardened to the formulas of confession or skeptical about himself. "In the first confession," he says, "a convert really believes in his own promises."[5]

Not far in the past these disciples had made some promises. No doubt they really believed in those promises, and they gave purpose to their lives. They had a reason for living. They had work to do, tasks to accomplish. But the events of that dark Friday altered all that. They had made promises of allegiance, but the One to whom they had made the promises was not around any more. He had called them to be with him and to work with him, but he had now been removed from the scene and the mission on which they had embarked now seemed futile.

What was there for them to do now? Maybe they had been foolish to leave their homes, families, and jobs to become followers of this itinerant preacher/teacher who had now been executed as a criminal. Wise or foolish, there was now little point to the vows they had made. The purposes that had once given direction to their lives were dying away.

Then came the news that Joseph's tomb had not been adequate for the task assigned it. At first this seemed an idle tale, but after its truth was validated by their own encounter with the living Christ, those purposes began to be renewed and to grow strong again. They still had a living Lord. He still had work for them to do, and they had "miles to go" and "promises to keep."[6]

104

Lighting Darkened Tombs

In time this idle tale lightened up a darkened future, too. At the moment, the disciples may not have been greatly concerned about what was going to happen to Christ or to them beyond the experience of death. They had shared with others the belief in a resurrection at the end of the age. Such a belief depended upon trust in God. But after what had happened to Jesus, their faith must have been shaken terribly, and the tomb of death became darker than ever.

Can we be satisfied with a darkened tomb that has no exit? Can we be satisfied with that, especially for those we love? What does it do to our conception of life itself to believe that it simply ends and that that is all there is to it?

When Sigmund Freud's beautiful daughter, Sophia, died of influenza, he was so numbed by the sudden tragedy that he could only say unbelievingly, "She was blown away as if she had never been."[7] Her influence may have lived on in his life and in the lives of others, but what about that terrible darkness at the end of her life?

Leo Tolstoy lost three children and two aunts by death during the four years he was writing his novel, *Anna Karenina*. The novel is permeated with the question of meaning in the face of death. One of his biographers says: "Tolstoy had reached the farthest point to which his intelligence and imagination could take him as an observer of life, and there he found only one meaningful question: When one recognizes the inevitability of death, how can he go on living?"[8]

The news the disciples at first called an idle tale can help, because it points to a dazzling light in an empty tomb. All is not darkness in the mysterious region of death. There is a light in the darkness, and it speaks of life and joy!

After more than twenty centuries, some still call the news of Christ's resurrection an idle tale. But many others, in every century since the news was first announced, have been convinced, because of their own encounter with the living Christ, that it is truth and not nonsense. It is not a mockery of empty hearts to talk about a risen Christ.

105

This news is an invitation to let a dream take hold of us. We can live in companionship with One who talked about a kingdom where God's will would be done on earth as it is done in heaven. We need to be possessed by that dream.

This Christ who now speaks on the resurrection side of that garden tomb calls us to loyalty to him, to service in his name. Even when our commitment becomes weak and slack, he keeps calling us to faithfulness and purposeful devotion to him.

And because death could not hold him, there is light in the darkness at the end of the road. So we can have hope of life, abundant and eternal, both now and beyond the event of death.

He is risen! That is no idle tale. It is truth, glorious, wonderful truth!

------

1. Helen Keller, *The Open Door* (New York: Doubleday & Co., Inc., 1957), p. 47.

2. William Manchester, *The Death of a President* (New York, Evanston, London: Harper & Row Publishers, 1967), p. 748.

3. Edgar A. Guest, "Dreams," in *Collected Verse* (Chicago: The Reilly & Lee Co., 1934), p. 670.

4. Edwin Markham, "The Dream."

5. Graham Greene, *A Sort of Life* (New York: Simon and Schuster, 1971), p. 169.

6. Robert Frost, "Stopping by Woods on a Snowy Evening," in *The Poetry of Robert Frost*, edited by Edward Connery Lathem (New York, Chicago, San Francisco: Holt, Rinehart and Winston, Inc., 1969), pp. 224-225.

7. Francine Klagsbrun, *Sigmund Freud* (New York: Franklin Watts, Inc., 1967), pp. 85-86.

8. Morris Philipson, *The Count Who Wished He Were a Peasant* (New York: Pantheon Books, 1967), pp. 85-86.

16.

The Twice-Traveled Road

Luke 24:13-35

"Now on the same day two of them were going to a village called Emmaus, about seven miles from Jerusalem ... Jesus himself came near and went with them." — Luke 24:13-15

Two people, possibly a husband and wife, had been in Jerusalem during that tragic weekend when Jesus was crucified, and now had decided to return to their home. They lived in the village of Emmaus, about seven miles from Jerusalem. But what a long walk that must have seemed that day! They walked with heavy hearts, with so much on their minds.

Maybe that was one reason why they did not recognize this man who joined them on the road and walked along with them. Maybe they did not recognize him because they had no expectation of seeing him, or they were blinded by their grief. Preoccupation can cloud one's mind and affect one's vision; were they so preoccupied with their sorrow and the perplexing news of the empty tomb that their powers of recognition were made dormant?

We don't know the reasons for their not recognizing him; we only know that they did not. It was a Stranger who was walking with them, someone they did not know. Yet they felt comfortable enough with him to share the deepest concern of their lives as they walked along together.

The Road Away From What Might Have Been

These two people, leaving Jerusalem, were walking away from what might have been. "But we had hoped that he was the one to redeem Israel," they said to this Stranger.

That was what might have been, but was not. During much of their long history, the Hebrew people had been subject to other nations. They had known very little real freedom. But for centuries they had been longing for such, and cherishing the hope that a king would arise who would lead them to victory over their enemies and establish a strong and righteous nation for them. Like Ernest in Hawthorne's story of "The Great Stone Face," they had thrilled with anticipation as one person after another came along seeming to possess the possibilities of the deliverance they longed for. But again and again their hopes had been demolished.

The hopes revived once again when Jesus began his public ministry. Surely now the Redeemer of Israel had really come. At one point, the Gospel of John tells us, some "were about to come and take him by force to make him king" (John 6:15). Others became disillusioned when they realized that Jesus had other goals and purposes than the ones they held. Then when his enemies put him to death, the last bit of hope to which they had clung died with him. "We had hoped that he was the one to redeem Israel," but he wasn't. So two days after his crucifixion, these friends started home, walking away from what might have been.

Is that experience foreign to you? Have you never found yourself walking away from what might have been?

Here is a relationship that might have been beautiful, enriching, fulfilling, but something happens and you are left with only the shattered hope of what might have been. A baby is born, and two parents are filled with joy until they realize that their child will never have a healthy body or a normal mind. From then on they have to live with the broken dream of what might have been. Or the child grows into youth or young adulthood, and somehow the parents' commendable values and goals never become his or hers. The consequences are deplorable, perhaps even tragic, and the parents walk the road to Emmaus nursing the fractured dreams of what might have been.

So often events outside your control touch and change your life. An accident occurs, a disease strikes, a crime is committed, and life is never the same again. Things might have been so different, but

108

that possibility is gone now, and you are walking away from what might have been.

As a young man Jesse Stuart was a creative and innovative educator in the mountains of his native Kentucky. But he ran into so much opposition that after a few years he found himself jobless and had to leave Kentucky to get a job in education. He wrote that as he crossed the Mason-Dixon Line, his ideas of helping to educate his own people "were shineless stars in a background of memory."[1] He was walking away from what might have been.

That's part of what this Stranger encountered on the road to Emmaus: broken dreams, frustrated hopes, two people walking away from what might have been.

A Road Walked In Perplexity

Those two disciples were walking not only in disappointment; they were walking also in perplexity. "What are you discussing with each other while you walk along?" this Stranger asked the disciples. They were so flabbergasted they stopped, "looking sad." One of them, whose name was Cleopas, asked, "Are you the only stranger in Jerusalem who does not know the things that have taken place there in these days?" The Stranger responded, "What things?" They told him then about Jesus being crucified and about the unconfirmed news of the empty tomb.

They did not know what to believe about this. In their minds there was a mixture of hope and fear, of bewilderment and wonder, of love and grief, of doubt and faith.

So much of life is like that. It is filled with ambiguity, indefiniteness, uncertainty, and sometimes that is disconcerting, maybe even painful. Life would be so much simpler if we never had to be uncertain about anything.

That is one reason why Adolf Hitler had the power he did. He spoke with definiteness, with authority. He was both passionate and dogmatic. You did not have to wonder what to think or to do; he told you. And soon a whole nation was under the spell of his personality and his mind.

That is also why some religious leaders, who are out on what some of us call the fringes, attract people as they do. There is no wavering in their message. They speak as if they know exactly what the truth is, what everybody ought to do, and what is necessary to create the kind of world they think we ought to have. They leave no room at all for differences of opinion. They give no indication of thinking they might be wrong about anything, and many, wanting that kind of certainty, latch on to everything they say.

But life is not always that simple, the issues are not always that clear, the answers are not always that definite. This means that we often have to live with perplexity, with uncertainty, with ambiguity. This is not to say that there is no place for conviction and definiteness of belief. But it is to say that we should never be surprised or disturbed when we discover within ourselves a blending of faith and doubt, of love and grief, of hope and fear, of bewilderment and wonder.

All of this was within those two disciples going from Jerusalem to Emmaus that day, and may very well be within us today, too.

Companionship On The Road

But then something happened on that road that changed their lives forever. The living Christ joined them and walked and talked with them. For the rest of the way, they walked that road in companionship with him. It was only later that they realized the full significance of what had happened, but even then they sensed that something momentous was taking place.

At first they did not know who he was. In fact, not until they had reached their destination and had sat down to eat together did they realize who their Companion had been. Then as they thought about that walk, they said, "Were not our hearts burning within us while he was talking to us on the road, while he was opening the scriptures to us?"

The idea of "burning hearts" may have negative connotations for us, but it did not for these persons. For them it was more like what John Wesley meant when he wrote of his heart being "strangely warmed." On that walk they had experienced a quality of fellowship that had a lifting, renewing, enervating influence in their lives.

110

That was because of what Christ brought with him. He did not come, as he never comes, with empty hands. He brought instruction, for one thing. He opened the scriptures to them so that they saw them in a new light. The scriptures came to have meaning for them they had never had before.

But he brought more than instruction. He brought himself. True, for a time they did not know it was he, but still he blessed them. They did not know who he was, but they knew he was giving them something they very much needed.

Graham Greene tells about a man who could come into a room full of people and you wouldn't notice his coming, but you would notice that the whole atmosphere of a discussion had quietly altered, and that even the relations of one guest to another had changed. He says that no one any longer would be talking for effect, and "when you looked round for an explanation, there he was — complete honesty born of complete experience had entered the room and unobtrusively taken a chair."[2]

Something like this, only infinitely greater, had happened when Jesus joined those two people on the road from Jerusalem to Emmaus. They thought he did not know what they knew, but before long they sensed that the very atmosphere of their lives was being changed. They still didn't know it, but he was the One they had hoped would redeem Israel; now they found themselves being redeemed. He had been raised from death; now he was raising them from another kind of death to a new kind and quality of life.

A Road Traveled With Good News

I wonder if anywhere on that road between Jerusalem and Emmaus these disciples asked this Stranger who he was. Perhaps not. But when they sat down to eat together and Jesus blessed and broke bread for them, they suddenly realized who he was. He was the Friend they had lost, their Lord who had been crucified, and now he had been raised to new life.

Then all of a sudden he was gone, "vanished out of their sight." What did they do then? Begin to nurse their wounds again, to doubt the reality of what had happened? No, they were so excited that they just had to share their good news with others. So they started

111

back to Jerusalem! It was seven miles or more, but that didn't matter. They had wonderful news to share with dear friends, and the lateness of the hour and the distance to be traveled were irrelevant.

When they arrived in Jerusalem, they "found the eleven and their companions gathered together." They were told, "The Lord has risen indeed, and he has appeared to Simon!" Then these travelers shared their good news: "They told what had happened on the road, and how he had been made known to them in the breaking of bread."

They realized that what had happened was not for private consumption, but was good news to be shared with anyone who would listen. I wonder if they remembered that story in their scriptures where four leprous men had found a besieging army's camp deserted but with plentiful rations left behind. At first they had thought to hide and hoard as much as they could for themselves, but then they came to the realization that this news needed to be shared. So they said, "This is a day of good news; if we are silent and wait until the morning light, we will be found guilty; therefore let us go and tell the king's household." And they did (2 Kings 7).

I don't know whether they thought about that story, or not. But I do know they realized this news had to be shared. So the road they had just walked, in disappointment, in perplexity, traveling away from what might have been, they now walked with a lighter and quicker step because they had glorious good news to tell. And from that time until this, people who have come to know the living Christ have traveled all kinds of roads sharing that good news with others.

---

1. Jesse Stuart, *The Thread That Runs So True* (New York: Charles Scribner's Sons, 1949, 1958), p. 270.

2. Graham Greene, *Ways of Escape* (New York: Washington Square Press, 1963; copyright 1980 by Graham Greene), pp. 26-27.

17.

The Identifying Scars

Luke 24:36-43; John 20:24-29

"And when he had said this, he showed them his hands and his feet." — Luke 24:40; cf. John 20:20

On his pilgrimage to the Celestial City, in John Bunyan's *The Pilgrim's Progress*, Faithful is overtaken by a man who mauls and batters him mercilessly. He is unable to resist his strength, so he pleads with him to have mercy upon him. But the strong man answers, "I know not how to show mercy," and knocks him down again.

Later, in relating this experience to Christian, Faithful says, "He had doubtless made an end of me, but that one came by and bid him forbear."

"Who was that that bid him forbear?" Christian asks, and Faithful answers: "I did not know him at first; but as he went by I perceived the holes in his hands and his side; then I concluded that he was our Lord."[1]

Those were the marks and proofs of his identity on which Christ himself relied. In helping his friends to recognize him after his resurrection, he did not call attention to the features of his face nor to the color of his eyes or his hair nor to the size or shape of his body. Instead, he said, "Look at my hands and my feet; see that it is I myself." Then "he showed them his hands and his feet" (the Gospel of John says that he showed them his side, too). By those scars they recognized him as their crucified and risen Lord.

Those scars were the marks of identity for which the disciples were looking. Indeed, Thomas said that he would not believe that

113

Jesus was alive until he had seen and felt his scars. No doubt others felt the same. But Jesus did not condemn them for this. In fact, it appears that it was his scars that he was most anxious for them to see. The reason must surely have been that they had more to say than any other of his identifying characteristics.

Those scars still possess a matchless eloquence, and we in our day, no less than those first disciples, need to see them and to hear their message.

Symbols Of Victory

I hear them speaking of victory. They are symbols of victory. The wounds which were supposed to defeat and destroy have healed, and only the scars remain as testimony to victory over the forces of evil that inflicted the wounds.

When those holes were made in Jesus' hands and feet and side, it seemed that the forces of evil were in control. Their hour of triumph had come. But the triumph was short-lived. Their victory did not last long, and when Jesus showed his disciples his scars, he was affirming his victory over the forces of evil.

In writing about an interview with the late poet, Robert Frost, a reporter gave a vivid description of his appearance: his white, silky hair that tended to sift down to the left side of his forehead; his pale blue eyes and craggy eyebrows; his thick, slightly jutting lower lip; his over-all rough-hewn granite likeness. Then he noted that Frost had had what he called "an altercation with a surgeon" which had left a slight scar on his right cheek. "But the real scar," the reporter said, "is the scar of living, and no man ever wore it more proudly or with more stunning effect."[2]

Jesus, too, wore "the scar of living," and in his life, as in the lives of many in our day, that scar witnessed to victories won. But the scars he showed his disciples after his resurrection were the scars of dying. They were the scars that resulted from human efforts to destroy him. But by his resurrection those efforts had been frustrated.

In a dramatic poem, Theodosia Garrison imagines two soldiers talking as they come down the "hill of Calvary." One is thinking only of how long it takes these thieves to die. The other admits to being sorely afraid, but not knowing why. She also sees two women weeping as they come down the hill. One is angry and declares that "men shall rue this deed their hands have done." The other can only say through her tears, "My son! My son! My son!" The poet hears two angels singing, too. One declares, "Death is vanquished," and the other sings, "Love hath conquered all, O heaven and earth rejoice!"[3]

He was battered and bruised, but he won the victory. Those scars are symbols of victory. So today when it seems that right is on the scaffold and wrong is on the throne, we need not sink into despair. We need, rather, to look again at the Master's scars. They assure us that he has dealt a death blow to the forces of evil. Their doom is sealed. Victory belongs to our God!

Proofs Of Love

Those scars speak also of love. They are proofs of Christ's love. "No one has greater love than this, to lay down one's life for one's friends" (John 15:13). If Jesus' disciples had ever had any doubt of his love for them, the sight of those scars should have dispelled that doubt. There was indisputable evidence of his love.

Dr. Harry A. Fifield, who for many years was pastor of the First Presbyterian Church in Atlanta, once told of standing as a boy with his mother waiting for a trolley, when a strange-looking woman walked by. An ugly scar marred one whole side of her face, and he thought she was the ugliest person he had ever seen. To his surprise, his mother spoke to her, and the ugly woman smiled back with a smile that seemed not to fit her face at all. After she passed by, he asked his mother who she was. She told him her name, and then said, "She's a lovely woman, and she used to be very pretty. But one day her house caught fire, and she was horribly burned saving her baby from the flames. That's why her face is so scarred."

Dr. Fifield said that he kept looking back to catch another glimpse of that woman. Although he was not old enough to understand why, she was suddenly lovely to his eyes. Later he realized that her scars were the marks of a love that had paid a tremendous price to manifest itself.

Jesus' scars are like that. They speak more eloquently than words of a love that does not count the cost, but goes all the way to the cross to manifest itself. Charles Wesley exclaimed: "O Love divine, what hast thou done! / The immortal God hath died for me!"[4] If in Jesus we see who God is, it is no wonder that John said, "God is love" (1 John 4:8). Jesus' scars tell us that. They are proofs of Divine love.

Tokens Of Sympathy

That means then that they are also tokens of sympathy and understanding. They tell us that we do not have a remote God, unacquainted with the difficult experiences of life. Rather, Christ who is the Word made flesh (John 1:14) was himself "tested by what he suffered," and so is able to sympathize and "to help those who are being tested" now. This, the writer of the Letter to the Hebrews says, should encourage us to "approach the throne of grace with boldness, so that we may receive mercy and find grace to help in time of need" (Hebrews 2:17-18; 4:14-16).

A few years ago, journalist Cynthia B. Astle had surgery for thyroid cancer. After she had completed radiation therapy and had been released by her physicians, she wrote an article under the title, "We'll Know We Are Christians by Our Scars." She began the article by saying, "Lately my mail has been full of blessed scars." These, she said, were the scars various persons had written to tell her about as they offered her messages of encouragement and hope and promises of prayer. As she had reflected upon her own experience and upon those shared with her by others, she had come to the conclusion that "the reality of God is most often revealed when we show one another the scars that divine love has healed and redeemed." Then she said, "After all, it is by his wounds that we recognize the Risen Christ."[5]

We can believe more surely in others' understanding and sympathy when we know that they, too, have been wounded. Wounds tend to increase the capacity to understand, to empathize, to sympathize.

James M. Barrie is best known as the creator of Peter Pan, the boy who refused to grow up. Barrie was terribly shocked at the

116

age of six by the death of his brother and the impact this had upon his mother. He later said that that was where his mother got her soft eyes and why other mothers ran to her when they had lost a child. They knew she understood.

When life becomes difficult for us, when pain and heartache become our lot, we need to look at the Master's scars and remember again that he has been through the worst and therefore understands. His scars are tokens of sympathy and understanding.

Claims Of Allegiance

We must not forget though that those scars are also claims of allegiance. They are Christ's authority for demanding our loyalty. He suffered those wounds for us, and he should have to do nothing more to win our allegiance than to show us his scars.

The saintly missionary, Amy Carmichael, who knew far more than her share of suffering, asked: "No wound? No scar?" Are we not supposed to be like the Master whose feet were pierced? "We follow a scarred Captain," she said, so should not we, too, have scars? Then she said: "Lest we forget, Lord, when we meet, / Show us Thy hands and feet."[6]

How those scars condemn us! Our half-hearted ventures of service, our reluctant offers of loyalty, our cowardly denials make us unworthy even to look upon those scars!

It is said that Saint Francis of Assissi had a vision once of the love of God crucified on a cross that stretched across the whole horizon. When the vision faded, he looked and discovered that the marks of nails were in his own hands, and he bore those marks to the end of his days.

I am not sure whether that is fact or legend, but I do know that when the Apostle Paul wanted to present undeniable evidence of Christ's ownership of his life, he pointed to the scars his body had accumulated during his years of service for Christ and said, "I carry the marks of Jesus branded on my body" (Galatians 6:17).

There is an old legend about Satan appearing to a saint once and declaring, "I am the Christ." But the saint confounded him by asking, "Where are the marks of nails?"

Could it be that when we glibly profess our allegiance to Christ, he replies, "Where are the marks of nails?" Not many of us — at least in our American world — are likely to receive physical wounds because of our loyalty to Christ, but his scars should prevent us from seeking an easy discipleship. Those scars are claims of allegiance.

Lord, when I am weary with toiling,
And burdensome seem Thy commands,
If my load should lead to complaining,
Lord, show me Thy hands —
Thy nail-pierced hands, Thy cross-torn hands;
My Saviour, show me Thy hands!

Christ, if ever my footsteps should falter,
And I be prepared for retreat,
If desert or thorn cause lamenting,
Lord, show me Thy feet —
Thy bleeding feet, Thy nail-scarred feet;
My Jesus, show me Thy feet!

Oh, God, dare I show Thee
My hands and my feet?[7]

1. John Bunyan, *The Pilgrim's Progress* (London and Glascow: Collins, 1953; Part I originally published in 1678 and Part II in 1684), pp. 84-85.

2. Edward Connery Lathem, editor, *Interviews with Robert Frost* (New York, Chicago, San Francisco: Holt, Rinehart and Winston, 1966), p. 185.

3. Theodosia Garrison, "I Heard Two Soldiers Talking," copyright 1971 by Art Masters Studios, Inc., Minneapolis, Minnesota.

4. Charles Wesley, "O Love Divine, What Hast Thou Done," in *The United Methodist Hymnal* (Nashville: The United Methodist Publishing House, 1989), Number 287.

5. Cynthia B. Astle, "We'll Know We Are Christians By Our Scars," in *The United Methodist Reporter*, November 7, 1997, p. 2.

6. Cited by Corrie Ten Boom in *Tramp for the Lord* (New York: Pillar Books edition, 1976; copyright 1974 by Corrie Ten Boom and Jamie Buckingham), p. 118.

7. Source unknown.

18.

The Dispelled Doubt

John 20:19-29

"Then (Jesus) said to Thomas, 'Put your finger here and see my hands. Reach out your hand and put it in my side. Do not doubt but believe.' Thomas answered him, 'My Lord and my God!' "
— John 20:27-28

In Herman Melville's novel, *Moby Dick*, the men hunting the sperm whale have failed in their first attempt to kill the whale. In the process, they have been thrown out of their boat, and the boat has been filled with water. They are able to get back into the boat, but the sea is ferocious and the ship to which they are supposed to return seems to be nowhere around. With darkness engulfing them, they fear for their lives. Finally they are able to light a lantern and one of the men holds it aloft. Melville writes: "There, then, he sat, holding up that imbecile candle in the heart of that almighty forlornness. There, then, he sat, the sign and symbol of a man without faith...."[1]

That is what we see in Thomas the Disciple in the wake of Jesus' resurrection: "the sign and symbol of a man without faith." Listen to him: "Unless I see the mark of the nails in his hands, and put my finger in the mark of the nails and my hand in his side, I will not believe." That's a man without faith!

But remember that Thomas was not present at the earlier time when Jesus appeared to the other disciples. What did Jesus do then? "He showed them his hands and his side!" Thomas was simply asking for the same kind of evidence the others had received. They had seen Jesus' scars; he wanted to see them too — and also to touch them.

121

Was that not a normal reaction? Who, in regard to any number of things, has not said, "I'll believe it when I see it"? Haven't we at some time wanted concrete evidence to support beliefs we held or wanted to hold? We may even have specified the evidence that would satisfy us. So we can identify with Thomas. Call him the Doubter, the Pessimist, the Skeptic, or whatever, still we can understand his wanting solid support for belief in Jesus' resurrection.

Yet the fact remains that at that time he was "a man without faith." But that is not what we see as the scene progresses. Doubt controls his mind at first, but then the moment comes when that doubt is dispelled and he exclaims, "My Lord and my God!"

Valuing Truth

Don't you think Thomas is to be commended for valuing and wanting to know the truth?

In Henrik Ibsen's play, *An Enemy of the People*, Dr. Stockman is convinced that the town's water supply has become contaminated, but when a town meeting is called to deal with the problem, no one will acknowledge that the problem exists. Dr. Stockman is disturbed, not just because of the danger posed by the contaminated water, but even more because of the moral corruption revealed by the people's wish "to build the town's prosperity on a quagmire of falsehood and deceit." The citizens try to silence him, but he declares that he will shout the truth at every street corner and publish it in other towns' newspapers. That makes it clear to his fellow citizens that he is intent on ruining the town. He says, "Yes, my native town is so dear to me that I would rather ruin it than see it flourishing upon a lie."[2]

Thomas could not possibly have imagined all that would result from the news of Jesus' resurrection. Yet even if he could have foreseen the dimensions of the movement that would be based upon that claim, he still would have been unwilling to affirm it himself unless he was convinced that it was true. He would not have wanted the Christian Church to "flourish upon a lie."

Implied here is a basic appreciation of the worth of truth. Thomas was not about to say, "If I can't know the truth, it won't matter

122

much; something else will do just as well." He believed it mattered radically whether the claims being made by his fellow disciples were true or untrue.

The Israeli novelist Igal Mossinsoh has written a novel about Judas Iscariot in which he has Judas escaping from Judea and sailing to another country and taking up residence there, rather than hanging himself as the Gospel of Matthew reports (Matthew 27:5). He assumes a false name, establishes himself in business and social circles, and lives an outwardly normal life until some traveling Christians come along and recognize him. Under the strain of the impending catastrophe that he anticipates, he becomes not only frightened, but confused about his identify as well. His wife Martha says to him, "You're mad." But he replies, "I am searching for some truth to hold onto, and I can't find it."[3]

Thomas knew that if Jesus' resurrection had actually occurred, that was a truth he and others could "hold onto," and he is to be commended for wanting to find out if the claim was really true.

Wanting First-Hand Belief

I have mixed feelings about his unwillingness to accept the word of the other disciples and to enter into their belief. Why did he doubt them? Did he suspect that the dim light of early morning and the thick tears of the women who went to Jesus' tomb prevented them from finding his body there? And these men — he knew them well; did he know them too well to believe them in something as momentous as this?

He certainly was not beyond being influenced in his religious beliefs by other persons. No doubt that kind of influence had been coming to bear upon his life from his earliest days. He might have carved out a few of his beliefs on his own, but the chances are that most of them — certainly before he met Jesus — had come to him by way of loved ones and friends who had possessed them before he did.

In Tennyson's poem, "The Holy Grail," a young woman who has been privileged to see the cup from which Christ drank at the Last Supper is trying to convince Sir Galahad of the Grail's existence and of the possibility of his seeing it. Tennyson writes:

... and as she spake
She sent the deathless passion in her eyes
Thro' him, and made him hers, and laid her mind
On him, and he believed in her belief.

Do not many of our beliefs come to us in this same way — though not so dramatically or romantically? Few of us really pioneer in the matter of religious beliefs; rather, we believe in someone else's belief. But I have to admire Thomas for not being willing in so weighty a matter to settle for a second-hand faith. Had he not pushed on beyond the word of the other disciples until the resurrection faith became a reality of his own experience, he would have remained spiritually impoverished and impotent, never really possessing a faith of his own.

Seeking Sensible Evidence

Thomas was looking for evidence, and at the moment the only evidence that appeared acceptable to him was that attestable to the senses: "Unless I see the mark of the nails in his hands, and put my finger in the mark of the nails and my hand in his side, I will not believe."

Who would deny that it is tremendously important to be able to see and hear and touch and smell and taste? To lose one of these senses would take something valuable from one's life. But dare we go beyond that and say that only that is real which is attestable to the senses?

When Jesus appeared to Thomas that day, he made it clear that belief in his resurrection would never be dependent upon the senses. After Thomas had made his declaration of faith, Jesus said to him: "Have you believed because you have seen me? Blessed are those who have not seen and yet have come to believe." He was talking about us, if we have come to believe. But especially in this age of science and technology, like Thomas, we may want visible evidence, tangible proof, before we will believe in something as incredible as resurrection.

Saint Augustine, before his conversion, stumbled over this very thing. He said that he wanted to be as assured of things he could

124

not see as he was that seven and three add up to ten. God, surely, is not unsympathetic with that kind of feeling. After all, Jesus himself talked about knowing the truth and being set free by it (John 8:32).

Yet he knew that evidence that satisfies the senses is not the only, nor perhaps even the best, evidence there is. Who has ever seen love — not its expression, but the thing itself? Yet many of us know it to be "the greatest thing in the world."[4] Who has ever tasted goodness or touched peace of mind or smelled joy or heard sorrow? Life is so much more than meets the senses, and the person who does not realize that is deluded indeed!

Finding Proofs Unneeded

It is interesting to note that Thomas finally did not need the proofs he initially demanded. When Jesus appeared to him, he offered to let him believe according to the terms he had dictated: "Put your finger here and see my hands. Reach out your hand and put it in my side." But Thomas, without using the offered proof, cried out, "My Lord and my God!"

In so many areas of our lives, it turns out that we don't really need or even want what we thought we had to have. We set our hearts on some acquisition or goal or dream. We think it is essential to our happiness or fulfillment that we get what we are wanting. We may get it and then discover that it does not do for us what we thought it would do. Or we may not get it and still find that life does not cave in upon us.

Similarly in the area of faith, we may think it would all be so much clearer, that it would be easier to believe, if certain circumstances prevailed or particular proofs were available. And then one day, through the gracious initiatives of God, we find ourselves believing in spite of the absence of the conditions or terms we have wanted to dictate.

At age 22, novelist and playwright Graham Greene took instructions from a Catholic priest, mainly to please the girl he was planning to marry. At the time he had no intention of being received into the Church. There were too many obstacles in the way of belief for him to take that step. But after a time, he did take it. In his autobiography, *A Sort of Life*, he tells of a friend who was attending her father's funeral when an old priest who had known her as a child tried to persuade her to return to the Church. At last, to please him more than for any other reason, she said, "Well then, Father, remind me of the arguments for the existence of God." After a long hesitation, he admitted to her, "I knew them once, but I have forgotten them." Greene says, "I have suffered the same loss of memory. I can only remember that in January 1926 I became convinced of the probable existence of something we call God ... and my belief never came by way of those unconvincing philosophical arguments."[5]

This is not to say that good, hard thinking is inappropriate; it is very much in order. But how seldom it is that we arrive at belief by the route we think necessary, and how unessential the proofs we thought to be absolutely necessary may become when through encounter with the living Christ, he becomes a reality in our lives.

At least one theological reason for this is that the initiative for creating such belief always rests with God, and in reaching us and nudging us on to redeeming faith, God is not restricted to the methods we may try to devise or prescribe. Browning put it like this:

> *Just when we are safest, there's a sunset touch,*
> *A fancy from a flower-bell, someone's death,*
> *A chorus-ending from Euripides,*
> *And that's enough for fifty hopes and fears*
> *As old and new at once as nature's self,*
> *To rap and knock and enter in our soul ...*

Well, where does this bring us? It brings us to realization that the proofs we had thought most essential may not be so important after all; to assurance that we may not be as secure in our doubts as we had thought; and to expectation of experience of the resurrected Christ, not because we are so determined in our seeking, but because he is so gracious in his finding. And we may find ourselves believing for strange new reasons, perhaps not related at all to the ones we had thought to be so indispensable. Then with doubt dispelled, we hear ourselves declaring with conviction and joy, "My Lord and my God!"

1. Herman Melville, *Moby Dick; or The Whale,* Great Books of the Western World edition (Chicago, London, Toronto, Geneva: Encyclopaedia Britannica, Inc., 1952), Vol. 48, p. 167.

2. Henrik Ibsen, "An Enemy of the People," in *Gateway to the Great Books,* edited by Robert M. Hutchins, Mortimer J. Adler, and Clifton Fadiman (Chicago, London, Toronto, Geneva: Encyclopaedia Britannica, Inc., 1963), Vol. 4, p. 227.

3. Igal Mossinsoh, *Judas,* translated from the Hebrew by Jules Harlow (New York: St. Martin's Press, 1963), p. 206.

4. The title of Henry Drummond's classic little book on 1 Corinthians 13.

5. Graham Greene, *A Sort of Life* (New York: Simon and Schuster, 1971), pp. 167-168.

19.

The Propelling Word

Matthew 28:16-20; Mark 16:12-18; Luke 24:44-49; Acts 1:6-11

"Go therefore and make disciples of all nations, baptizing them in the name of the Father and of the Son and of the Holy Spirit, and teaching them to obey everything that I have commanded you."
— Matthew 28:19-20

On Christmas Eve of 1784, about sixty Methodist preachers met in a little church in Baltimore, Maryland, to organize the Methodist Episcopal Church in America. Theirs was a momentous and historic gathering, but they completed their work within ten days. Their real task, they knew, was waiting for them outside the walls of that church building, in the settled communities and on the frontiers of a new nation. When the meeting was over, those preachers, most of them under thirty years of age, leaped on their horses and rode off to their various appointments to take the gospel of Christ to people everywhere they could find them. It was almost as if they were being propelled by a power outside themselves.

But they were not the first to be propelled across the earth in the name of Christ. They stood rather in a long line that reaches all the way back to first century Palestine. The Risen Lord said to those first disciples of his, "Go therefore and make disciples of all nations," and the Gospel of Mark says, "They went out and proclaimed the good news everywhere" (Mark 16:20).

Geographical boundaries were ignored by these men: "They proclaimed the good news everywhere" — and also to everyone. They had not detected any social or racial restrictions in the command of

129

their Risen Lord. Indeed, they were commanded to take the gospel to "all nations." For a people whose religious life had involved separation from others for the sake of acceptability to God, this was not an easy command to understand or accept. But before many years had gone by, one of the proudest of their number was writing to people who lived in the capital city of the Roman Empire, "I am a debtor both to Greeks and to barbarians, both to the wise and to the foolish — hence my eagerness to proclaim the gospel to you also who are in Rome" (Romans 1:14-15). The word "go" was propelling with such force that social and racial distinctions were being obliterated.

How do you explain this propulsion? How could there be such power in a two-letter word?

A Word From Their Risen Lord

There could not have been such power, at least for these men, if the word had come from some other person. Just anyone could not have had that kind of power over them. When they were told to "go," they went because they recognized the authority of the One who had spoken to them.

Why do we so frequently ask, "Who said this?" when we are evaluating something we have heard. We ask it because its reliability depends so heavily upon its source. And when we are trying to decide whether or not to do something we have been told to do, why are we so interested in knowing who told us to do it? Because the authority of the command depends so wholly upon the one who gave it. No person can afford to recognize just any authority. One has to decide whose voice will be authoritative in his or her life.

The disciples had done that, though many around them thought they had made a stupid choice. There were others they could have chosen to obey: the emperor, kings, governors, religious officials, local authorities. But they chose instead to take their orders from a Galilean carpenter turned itinerant preacher, teacher, and healer, who was executed on a cross like a common criminal. What poor judgment they had, many of their contemporaries thought.

Centuries earlier when Moses was trying to rescue his people from their slavery in Egypt, he asked the Pharaoh, in the name of the Lord, to let the people go. But Pharaoh said, "Who is the Lord, that I should heed him and let Israel go? I do not know the Lord, and I will not let Israel go" (Exodus 5:1-2).

Even many who had seen Jesus would have said, as Pharaoh did, "I do not know the Lord." His word held no authority for them. But it did for this handful of people who had come to think of him as their Lord, their Master, their Savior. During the months they had journeyed with him, they had seen such tender compassion, such untarnished love, such sane judgment, that his word had become their command. If he said "Go," they would go, and nothing would stop them!

He still has that kind of authority today in the lives of those who have come to know his gracious love and his saving power.

A Word That Pointed To A Needy World

Notice that this is a word that, if obeyed, changes the focus of one's life, away from one's self toward others.

Once when the Apostle Paul had been "forbidden by the Holy Spirit" to proclaim the gospel in one place after another, he came to the city of Troas on the western edge of Asia. Tarrying there, he had a vision one night in which "there stood a man of Macedonia pleading with him and saying, 'Come over and help us'" (Acts 16:6-10).

Jesus said, "Go," and a perishing people pled, "Come over and help us." It is true that these evangelists were not welcomed everywhere. In fact, they and their message were frequently spurned. But again and again, as Jesus' word resounded in their hearts and minds, they heard other words uttered by a needy people, saying, "Come over and help us."

Jesus had talked about fields being "already white for the harvest" (John 4:35), and now those fields glistened before their eyes. But it was not a lovely sight to behold. Instead, for those who had come to know Christ, it was a sight that pained and disturbed and moved to action.

131

Yet not everyone saw the world as these commissioned men saw it. Some saw it simply as a likely place to gain a fortune or to have a merry time. Some saw the possibilities it provided for exploitation and the attaining of power. Its pain and heartache and tragedy and sorrow were of no consequence to them. But all was different for those who had come to know the spirit of the Living Christ.

The truth lay bare before them. They looked upon the same world that others saw, but they saw it in its need and desperation. They saw a world astray, in need of a Guide; hurt and in need of a Healer; hungry and in need of the Bread of Life; thirsty and in need of the Water that satisfies; perishing and in need of a Savior.

We could compare that world with the world in which we live and perhaps find some grounds for boasting, but still we would have to admit that ours, too, is an unredeemed world. Its desires are too selfish, its scale of values too warped, its conduct too unworthy. There is so much that is wrong in our world. Many, it is true, keep going along as if they have all they need, but from the depths of the hearts of vast numbers of people the plea still comes, "Come over and help us." Christ still says, "Go," and those who recognize the authority of his voice, if they listen, hear a multitude crying out, "Come."

A Word That Matched An Inward Impulse

Then, because of an impulse within that corresponds to the command and the plea from without, they publish their message and seek to fulfill their task.

When Jesus commissioned those first disciples, he was not ordering them to do something they did not want to do. Rather, he was appointing them to the task to which their hearts already impelled them. They had good news to tell, and it didn't take much urging to get them to tell it.

In 1773 John Wesley sent George Shadford to work with the young Methodist movement in America. His letter to him, just prior to his embarkation, was a brief but challenging one. He said:

"The time is arrived for you to embark for America.
You must go down to Bristol, where you will meet with

*Thomas Rankin, Captain Webb, and his wife. I let you
loose, George, on the great continent of America.
Publish your message in the open face of the sun, and
do all the good you can."*[1]

"I let you loose, George, on the great continent of America."
That's what Jesus was saying to his disciples that day. He was not
forcing them into a task; he was letting them loose with their message. They had a story to tell and a song to sing; he was saying,
"Tell your story and sing your song!"

We wonder if they would not have done it anyway. The Apostle
Paul once said, "If I proclaim the gospel, this gives me no ground
for boasting, for an obligation is laid on me, and woe to me if I do
not proclaim the gospel" (1 Corinthians 9:16). I think that was an
obligation he felt in the depths of his being. That was true of the
others as well. They had found a Friend too precious to hide, a
Savior too wonderful not to share. They would have been "utterly
miserable" if they had not told the good news. They either had to
go, or they had to forget about the Man who had brought so much
into their lives.

I like this story about the Protestant reformer Katherine Zell.
When she was charged with getting out of her place in sharing the
gospel — coming too near to preaching! — she said she knew she
could never be a member of the clergy, but she said, "I am like the
dear Mary Magdalene, who with no thought of being an apostle,
came to tell the disciples that she had encountered the risen Lord."[2]

That's what one person after another did, beginning with those
first disciples and continuing as others, too, all over the Roman
world, "encountered the risen Lord." They came to tell others the
good news.

Early on, when Peter and John were ordered by Jerusalem religious authorities to "speak no more to anyone" in the name of
Jesus, they replied, "Whether it is right in God's sight to listen to
you rather than to God, you must judge; for we cannot keep from
speaking about what we have seen and heard" (Acts 4:13-22).

A cartoonist pictures a minister leaning on his pulpit and saying to his congregation: "The question is: How do we win the world
to Christ ... with a minimum of fuss and bother?"[3]

Can you imagine those first disciples asking such a question as that? No! The command of their Lord held too much authority for them for that. He had too dear a place in their hearts for that.

Woodrow Wilson spent some of the choicest years of his life at Princeton University, first as a student, then as a professor, and finally as the president of the University. He had some difficult experiences there, yet for him Princeton was the "promised land" to which he yearned to return in the last years of his life. Biographer Arthur Walworth says that when he was lying at the gate of death, he said to one of his Princeton friends: "If they cut me open afterward, they'll find engraved on my heart — PRINCETON."[4]

CHRIST was the name engraved on the hearts of these first disciples who were propelled all across the Roman Empire with the good news of God's redeeming love displayed so surely and completely in Jesus Christ. They went wherever they went in his dear name.

When they looked around, they saw a world that desperately needed to hear the good news they had to tell, and their own experience of Christ and their love for him impelled them to go and tell others.

So may it be with us, too, for the word is still "GO"!

---

1. *The Works of John Wesley* (Grand Rapids, Michigan: Zondervan Publishing House; edition of 1872 authorized by the Wesleyan Conference Office, London), Vol. XII, p. 457.

2. Ruth Tucker, "Colorizing Church History," in *Christianity Today*, July 20, 1992, p. 21.

3. Cartoon by Doug Hall, in *Leadership*, Spring 1993, p. 24 (copyright 1993 by Doug Hall).

4. Arthur Walworth, *Woodrow Wilson* (Boston: Houghton Mifflin Company, 1958, 1965), Book One, p. 160.

20.

The Sustaining Promise

Matthew 28:16-20; Mark 16:12-18; Luke 24:44-49; Acts 1:6-11

"And remember, I am with you always, to the end of the age."
— Matthew 28:20

Bishop William R. Cannon used to say that he volunteered to be a preacher, and God accepted him and let him do it. I can't say that I volunteered for the job, but I never resisted the call as I have heard so many ministers say that they did. I was eighteen years old when the Quarterly Conference of Centralhatchee Methodist Church in Heard County, Georgia, recommended me to receive a License to Preach. This was on a Sunday afternoon in the early summer of 1947. The District Superintendent asked me if I wanted to say anything to the Conference. I don't know what I said, except for one thing: I said that I did not feel worthy or capable of being a minister, but that I was willing to do it because Jesus had said, "Lo, I am with you always, to the close of the age."[1]

That promise must have been precious to Jesus' first disciples also. It certainly came at a timely point in their experience with him. For three years his presence had been their life and joy. Then through some long, dark hours he had been away from them — gone forever, they thought — and life had seemed empty and meaningless to them. Now, so far as bodily presence was concerned, he was about to be away again. Besides that, he was setting a task before them that would require their greatest efforts and more. They could not do it if they had to do it alone. But they didn't. He was going to be with them. They had his word for it, and they knew he was a man of his word.

135

So it must have been with confidence — not in themselves, but in him — that they launched out on their mission. They were not going alone; their Lord and Master was going with them.

Providing Fellowship In Aloneness

This meant that they could be sure of fellowship in the midst of aloneness. There was no question as to whether they would experience aloneness; it was inevitable. The very nature of life itself made it inevitable. Matthew Arnold expressed it like this:

> Yes, in the sea of life enisled,
> With echoing straits between us thrown,
> Dotting the shoreless watery wild,
> We mortal millions live alone.[2]

Some would deny that life is really that way. But Jesus knew that those who sought to do his bidding would find themselves separated at times even from those who knew and loved them best. For some this would mean the chasm of physical distance, but the even more painful loneliness would be that caused by differences in thought, in aims and purposes, in desires and motives. Those who lived under the sway of Christ's influence would at times know a marvelous fellowship with others, but they might also experience the terrible isolation of deep commitment and dedicated living. There would be a sense in which they would be living in a different world from many of the people around them.

But they had this assurance: They would never, as long as they were true to Christ, be away from his presence. He had promised to be with them, and they knew that however isolated — physically, psychologically, spiritually — they might be from others, they could always count on his sustaining fellowship. That would put something into life for them that nothing else could.

Even today, the life of Christian devotion and service can be a lonely life at times, but Christ's promise of long ago is valid for us, too. "Remember," he said, "I am with you always." That means we may know his fellowship even in our aloneness.

Supplying Strength For Service

It also means strength for service. Those disciples had a gigantic task ahead of them. They could not do it alone. They needed strength beyond what they themselves possessed or could muster. Christ's promise to be with them encouraged them to believe that the strength would be there when they needed it.

In *An Enemy of the People*, Henrik Ibsen pictures a man who has stood for the right against the crowd and has suffered for his stand. His wife Katherine is afraid he will be driven out of the country, but he is not afraid, for he believes himself to be the strongest man in the town — perhaps, he says, "the strongest man in the whole world." The basis of this belief is a discovery he has made. "The strongest man in the world," he says, "is he who stands most alone."[3]

Surely, there is strength to be gained in standing alone, when that stand is for the right. But the strongest person in the world is not the one who stands most alone. Rufus Jones once said that one person alone is nobody at all! But if Christ is standing with one, that makes all the difference in the world.

The Apostle Paul had learned this through long experience in seeking to "make disciples of all nations." He had encountered all kinds of obstacles and opponents but had not been deterred from the mission Christ had given him. In writing to the church at Rome, he raised the question, "Who will separate us from the love of Christ?" Then he called the roll of things that might possibly do that: hardship, distress, persecution, famine, nakedness, peril, sword. Then he exclaimed, "No, in all these things we are more than conquerors through him who loved us!" But he wasn't through yet. He went on then to call yet another roll of enemies of the human spirit, declaring the doom of their efforts. He said, "For I am convinced that neither death, nor life, nor angels, nor rulers, nor things present, nor things to come, nor powers, nor height, nor depth, nor anything else in all creation, will be able to separate us from the love of God in Christ Jesus our Lord" (Romans 8:31-39).

No wonder Paul and his fellow missionaries gained a reputation for "turning the world upside down!" (Acts 17:6). If Christ was with them, they had strength for their task.

And so do we! The task is not yet completed — far from it. Now it is ours, and Christ is with us to give us strength to make disciples for him and to cooperate in the interests of the Kingdom of God.

Giving Direction For Action

Notice, too, that Christ's promise assured the disciples of direction for the living of their lives and the fulfilling of their mission. Here, again, there was no question as to their need for direction. They were going to be doing something neither they nor anyone else had ever done. How were they to know what to do? How could they carry out this mission? They needed a greater wisdom than their own.

When Lord Irwin was Viceroy of India, he and Mahatma Gandhi often had serious differences of view. One day a friend and supporter of Gandhi tried to ease the conflict between the two by saying, "Mahatma, you must know that Lord Irwin never makes a decision without praying over it first." Gandhi reflected on this for some moments and then said, "And why do you suppose God so consistently gives him the wrong advice?"[4]

There must surely have been times when friends, as well as opponents, thought Jesus' disciples had been given "the wrong advice." Indeed, the missioners themselves often disagreed with one another. A classic illustration of this occurred between Paul and Barnabas when they were getting ready for their "second missionary journey." Barnabas wanted to take John Mark with them, but Paul objected. The narrator of Acts tells us, "The disagreement became so sharp that they parted company" (Acts 15:36-41).

These folk made mistakes; they were not perfect. Yet within a generation they had taken the gospel of Christ all over the Roman Empire. They could not have done that in their own wisdom and strength alone, but Christ was with them, giving direction to their efforts.

Christ is always with those who are spreading the good news, taking the gospel to people who need to hear it. He does not save them from all mistakes, he does not deliver them from all errors of judgment. But somehow, when they are faithful, their efforts bear

138

fruit, the good news spreads, new disciples are made, and those who are already disciples are built up in the faith.

Bringing Blessing Out Of Trouble

One more thought: When Jesus promised to be with his disciples, that meant through bad times as well as good times, and consequently there were many instances when they found blessings where there had seemed to be only troubles.

Calvin Coolidge once observed to Herbert Hoover that if you see ten troubles coming down the road, you can be sure that nine will run into the ditch before they reach you and you will have to do battle with only one of them.[5]

That may be a good philosophy to live by. Who has never been guilty of anticipating troubles that never materialized? But those early Christians had their share of them. Luke tells us that some who were beaten because they would not agree to stop speaking in Christ's name "rejoiced that they were considered worthy to suffer dishonor for the sake of the name" (Acts 5:41). Paul and Silas sang in prison in Philippi (Acts 16:25), and years later, after a long imprisonment on two continents, Paul wrote to the Philippian Christians, "What has happened to me has actually helped to spread the gospel" (Philippians 1:12).

This gives us a clue to one reason why they could find blessings in their troubles: Their own welfare was not the chief good as they saw it. The spread of the gospel, the winning of persons to acceptance of Christ as Lord and Savior, was more important than what happened to them. When you get that kind of outlook upon life, personal troubles do not distress so much as before. Then, too, when one begins to look for traits of character and qualities of spirit instead of for material prosperity or social prominence, troubles are evaluated by the contribution they make to these, and not by the amount of suffering or inconvenience or embarrassment they have caused.

Through whatever becomes our lot, Christ assures us, he is with us, and if somehow our troubles make us more aware of him and more obedient to him, there cannot but be blessing in them.

The late Bishop Francis J. McConnell once wrote of his wife: "It may seem strange to use a term suggestive of mathematics in speaking of one's wife, but she is one of the 'constant quantities.' Having become a friend of anyone, she remains a friend forever."[6] Austin Farrer said something similar about C. S. Lewis. He said that when Mr. Lewis entered into any relationship, his patience and his loyalty were inexhaustible. He said, "He really was a Christian — by which I mean, he never thought he had the right to stop."[7]

Christ, too, "remains a friend forever." He is one of those "constant quantities." Indeed, he is the supreme constant quality, for he has given his word and never thinks he has "the right to stop." We can count on that. We have his word that he will be with us always, providing an enriching fellowship in our aloneness, supplying a strength that will make us "more than conquerors," giving us direction in a bewildered and bewildering world, and helping us to find blessings even in our troubles.

Those early Christians were sustained by that promise. So may we, too, be in this our day.

---

1. *King James Version* of Matthew 28:20.

2. Matthew Arnold, "To Marguerite."

3. Henrik Ibsen, "An Enemy of the People," in *Gateway to the Great Books*, edited by Robert M. Hutchins, Mortimer J. Adler, and Clifton Fadiman (Chicago, London, Toronto, Geneva: Encyclopaedia Britannica, Inc., 1963), Vol. 4, p. 246.

4. John Kenneth Galbraith, *Name-Dropping: From F.D.R. On* (Boston and New York: Houghton Mifflin Company, 1999), pp. 138-139.

5. Francis Russell, *The Shadow of Blooming Grove: Warren G. Harding in His Times* (New York and Toronto: McGraw-Hill Book Company, 1968), p. 616.

6. Francis J. McConnell, *By The Way* (New York and Nashville: Abingdon-Cokesbury Press, 1952), p. 81.

7. James T. Como, editor, *C. S. Lewis at the Breakfast Table* (New York: Macmillan Publishing Co., Inc., 1979), pp. 243-244.